Room to Grow

the Babycoach Guide to:

Independent sleep

Healthy eating

Discipline

By: Suzy Giordano

with

Marcella Giordano

First printing, March 2020

Copyright © 2020 by Books by Suzy and Marcella LLC

All rights reserved

The information contained here is not intended to replace the advice that you should receive from your doctor of other qualified health professional. Every child is different, and variation in care may be recommended based on individual circumstances. Always keep your pediatrician up to date.

Library of Congress cataloging-in-publication data has been applied for.

ISBN: 978-1-7345409-0-1

Printed in the United States of America

Without limiting the rights under copyright reserved above, no part of this publication may be reproduced, stored in or introduced into a retrieval system, or transmitted, in any form, or by any means (electronic, mechanical, photocopying, recording, or otherwise), without prior written permission of the copyright owner.

The scanning, uploading, and distribution of this book via the internet or via any other means without the permission of the copyright owner is illegal and punishable by law. Please purchase only authorized editions, and do not participate in or encourage electronic piracy of copyrighted materials. Your support of the authors' rights is appreciated.

While the authors have made every effort to provide accurate telephone numbers and Internet addresses at the time of publication, they do not assume responsibility for errors, or for changes that occur after publication.

To Allen Baxter, my husband, who makes me feel loved and important and Ava Isabelle, my Lily Beans. You have changed me for the better, expanded me. I love your laugh, your rare hugs and meaningful "I love you". Grandma loves you!

--Suzy Giordano Baxter

To Giorgio and Diana. My mom threw me into the deep end with you two. Penny and Emmanuel, thank you for taking a chance on me and trusting me with them! I spent three months, scared out of my mind, with you guys but in the end little Giorgio and lady Di proved my mom right. I'll always be grateful to you, who started it all, and all the others that came after.

--Marcella Giordano

Room
to
Grow

Contents

Foreword by Philip Floyd, M.D.

page v

Client Testimonials

page ix

Author Foreword

page xv

Introduction

page 1

Chapter One

The Babycoach Fundamentals

page 11

Chapter Two

Three to Six Months

page 21

Chapter Three

Six to Nine Months

page 41

Chapter Four

Nine to Twelve Months

page 59

Chapter Five

Twelve to Eighteen Months

page 77

Chapter Six

Eighteen to Twenty-Four Months

page 95

Chapter Seven

Twenty-Four to Thirty-Six Months

page 115

Chapter Eight

Three to Five Years

page 131

Chapter Nine

Five Years and Beyond

page 148

Chapter Ten

Nap Training

page 163

Chapter Eleven

Nightmares and Night Terrors

page 173

Chapter Twelve

Nutrition

page 177

Chapter Thirteen

Discipline

page 209

Chapter Fourteen

Frequently Asked Questions

page 219

Foreword

Suzy Giordano has done it again! She has given us unrivaled insight and direction into how to help our toddlers and young children sleep.

Sleep is a subject that is always on the radar, regardless of one's age or stage. We are constantly looking for ways to sleep more, to fall asleep more quickly, and to change our sleep hygiene in order to improve our quality of life.

But did you know that good sleep is of the highest import when it comes to young children? Scientists, physicians, and parents alike continue to evaluate this essential component of our young children's growth and well-being.

In all the research that has been done, a few important things are clear about our children's quality and quantity of sleep:

- They need more of it
- They don't function optimally without it
- It is an essential and integral part of their early childhood growth and development
- It has a significant impact on their emotional development
- The appropriate quantity improves their (and our) quality of life

According to the American Academy of Sleep Medicine and the American Academy of Pediatrics, sleeping, the recommended number of hours is associated with improved learning and memory, better attention, better emotional regulation and a better quality of mental and physical health.

So, how is good sleep achieved in young children? Well, I hope that's why you have chosen this book. Following in the brilliant approach found in her first book (12 Hour's Sleep by 12 Weeks Old), Ms. Giordano gives us a practical guide to making high quality sleep more than just a hope or aspiration; she helps us make it a reality.

I rarely recommend a book to parents of children in the early childhood years, largely because most books lack the practical information needed to support parents in raising their children. Not so when it comes to Suzy Giordano's book(s).

Since the time I first learned of Ms. Giordano's expertise, I have been recommending her books to the parents of newborns in my practice. I used her approach for all three of my children; it changed their lives – and ours. Her second book is a spectacular addition to my reading recommendations.

Parents and professionals, you need this book. Seize this opportunity to apply Ms. Giordano's practical insight and wisdom; you won't be disappointed.

Philip D. Floyd, MD, FAAP
President and Founder, Sunset Pediatrics, LLC, Miami, Florida
Clinical Assistant Professor of Pediatrics,
FIU Herbert Wertheim College of Medicine
Clinical Preceptor, NOVA Southeastern University College of Healthcare Sciences
Volunteer Clinical Faculty and Clinical Preceptor, Miami Children's Hospital
Medical Consultant, Miami-Dade County Public Schools

Client Testimonials

"It wouldn't be fair to describe Suzy as a sleep coach because her work is about much more than that. As first-time parents we were overwhelmed with all the new big ideas about how best to raise children. Suzy provided the clarity and the purpose to help us better navigate and enjoy our experience. Our son is not just sleeping much better -something we thought impossible- but he's also a more independent happier boy."

-Enrique and Florentina Acevedo

"Suzy and her team were with our family for just a few nights, but their legacy will last for many years. I know some children are natural born sleepers, but we were not so fortunate. It was clear that both needed to be taught how to sleep and neither my husband nor I possessed the capabilities. We were very conscious that something had to be done but felt equally strongly that whatever method we chose, it needed to be based in love and consistently provide appropriate comfort. Suzy's methods were the perfect fit. There is a process but there is also built-in flexibility that allows us to "stretch" the kids depending on our calendar. She taught our little ones how to navigate from a maximum of 2 hours of sleep at a time to between 10-12 per night. That's a gift for them and their own physical/mental development but if I'm being honest, that was also a gift to us as their parents. They wake up each morning rested and ready to tackle the day. And so, do we."

--Andrea in Washington, DC

"We have had the pleasure of working with Suzy to help all three of our children learn how to sleep. Suzy's wealth of knowledge, unparalleled experience and kind heart got us through some very difficult times. When Suzy came to help us with our youngest, he was waking every 2 hours at night and would only take naps outside in his stroller. With two other young children to run after and the frigid temperatures outside, this was not sustainable. My husband and I were exhausted, irritable and the worst version of ourselves (personally and professionally).

My feelings around Suzy's arrival for our 3 children were the same each time - hope and excitement mixed with nerves and fear. I knew what our family needed but I did not have the confidence to know we were going to get there. Suzy said to me "I have been over this bridge many times before and I know what lies on the other side. I am here to hold out my hand to you to help you get there." And hold out her hand she did. She helped us feel relaxed and confident armed with the knowledge that sleep is ever so crucial for every single member of our family. With her wealth of knowledge, she was able to tie a child's ability to learn to fall asleep and stay asleep to all aspects of parenting. As Suzy taught us, when your child learns to walk, there may be some bumps along the way but that does not mean we should keep them from learning what is developmentally appropriate and necessary. Suzy helped dispel all the chatter surrounding sleep, parenting, etc. so that we can focus on what matters most - a happy household with healthy children and parents who...SLEEP!

In addition to helping all 3 of our children, and therefore our family, learn to sleep, my husband and I picked Suzy's brain on all things parenting. Suzy has this amazing way of being absolutely loving and firm all at once. It was inspiring and helped us gain so much confidence as parents. I am forever grateful to Suzy for the immeasurable ways she has helped our family. My husband and I are confident knowing that we are providing our children with the very best and my children have confidence in their abilities to take on what once may have seemed to be a challenge."

--Annie Raykher

"I am a first-time mom, and my son was born December 2018. He will be four months. I read "Twelve Hours by Twelve Weeks" as it was recommended to me by a friend. It was the only baby book I read and wow I was not disappointed. I want to thank Suzy and the

Babycoach team for this book. All of the trainings went so smooth and my son sleeps 12 hours a night. Everyone is always so amazed when I tell them how well he sleeps. He has a great feeding and sleep schedule that we have been able to stick to. (Sometimes you need to be willing to wake a sleeping baby). Due to the way my son responded to the training; I can have peace of mind as a working mom as I return to work. Thank you so much for the teachings and trainings in your book. It works! I loved it and recommend it to all moms to be that I know."

--Stephanie Hoff Jackson, New Jersey

"My only regret is not hiring Suzy and her team earlier. She truly is a unicorn with magical powers. Prior to working with Suzy my son was waking up every 2-3 hours every night, often refused to take naps during the day, or took very short cat naps. Having him and his older brother who was also a toddler with no sleep was really impacting our lives. As a physician I really needed my sleep to function. My husband and I were both tired all the time, and the lack of sleep added huge amount of stress to our family life. We tried everything in the books to try to get him to sleep without luck which is why we hired Suzy and she was beyond amazing! By the time we hired her he was almost one year so really did not think he would be able to learn to sleep 12 hours a night but of course Suzy did it. She taught us how to put our son to sleep at night and gave him the skills to self soothe and put himself back to sleep. She also guided us after she left for nap training and he started taking two consistent naps every day.

She was always there even after she left and was a text away as she always answered any questions we had. Thanks to Suzy, life and order were restored – and I was able to focus on being a better mother to my sons. A big thank you to Suzy and her team!"

--A.K. Physician

"When my first daughter was born, I didn't know what I was in for. Thankfully, a dear friend recommended Suzy. 'You have to call Suzy', she said. 'Call her now!' This was when I was three months pregnant! What!?!? Done, and done.

Fast forward to when Carmen was born. I delivered via c-section. Suzy and Marcella were there from that first night I came home. I can't tell you how a) fortunate I feel that I could hire them to help me. And b) how reassuring it was to know they'd be there to help me when I got home-especially considering the pain I was in and our feelings of 'now what!?' They were literally an encyclopedia of knowledge on all things infant. I am historically a person who has suffered with anxiety and depression in the past. I went off my medication during pregnancy and was aware that childbirth could be a potentially triggering event that would rock my world. I was right. But without Suzy and Marcella it would have been overwhelmingly so. Giving birth isn't what it used to be. My family wasn't really around, and I needed tools. I needed taking care of as well. Suzy and Marcella's proven tactics were to get this infant on track for healthy habits. This helped me too. Healthy habits start with getting your infant on a consistent schedule of meals and naps. Happy mommy/daddy = happy baby!!

Suzy encourages independence on the baby's part. This seems counterintuitive but is essential and empowering for you and your baby. Someone once told me we raise our children to set them free. We begin this process when they are infants. It's a no fuss approach and may seem abrasive, but it's not. There is plenty of time in our lives to love on our children. They don't need to be sleeping in our beds too. Thank you, Suzy and Marcella, for giving us the tools so that our children sleep 10-12 hours a night in their cribs/beds. This allows us to watch things like Game of Thrones in peace and kick our feet up with a glass of wine-kid free! Congrats to the end of a successful day. Cheers to that!!

Priceless!"

--Kelly Mistretta. Washington D.C

Author Foreword

Here we go! After far too long, the follow up to my first book 12 Hours by 12 Weeks Old. I've learned so much over the past thirteen years. The Babycoach method has grown and evolved in ways that I could not have predicted but seem so obvious now with hindsight.

To be honest, the foundation of my method comes from a moment of my childhood that has stayed with me my whole life. For some reason or other, I found myself in trouble with my mother. Being the 60s in Brazil, corporal punishments were the norm. Luckily for me, that didn't really suit my parents. My mother was never the disciplinarian, rather she left that to my father. She loved to warn us that we would have to deal with him when he'd get home from work. That day, I pushed the boundaries and she didn't just warn me that she'd tell my dad, she actually did! I remember him walking in the door and her approaching him right away. He patiently listened to her report and stood there for a minute once her words had faded away. I was about 8 at the time, and I remember vividly that minute that he stood there lasted an eternity. He looked at me and told me to put on my shoes, that we were going for a walk. He turned and walked out the door pointing down to his side. Telling me without words where I was expected to be. We walked around the block. Any time I would try to make conversation or when my attention would start to wander, he'd shoot me a look. Not a mean one or one that left me fearful. Just a look that said "focus Suzy". After a few rounds around the block, he led me home. We sat in our family room and talked privately about what I had done.

As I grew older, I began to understand, that the longer the walk the deeper the trouble I was in. The time walking became less a punishment, something I was being made to do, and more an opportunity to think about what I had done and how I could've behaved better. It was only when I had children of my own that I began to understand what a powerful tool the walk was for my father. What a clever way for a parent to calm themselves and their child before responding. The walk gave my dad the opportunity to respond the way he wanted to, without anger or any other negative emotions. He could build us up and empower us to find ways to do better and not cut us down in the moment. A small strategy that would lay the foundation to my life's work.

What started as a way to get newborns sleeping through the night has grown into an overarching parenting philosophy that can be applied to all aspects of raising a child. I truly believe that if you are ready and willing to put in the work and be consistent, you will find the help you need in this book. You'll be able to lay the foundation to independent sleep, healthy eating, and discipline. This can be done at any age, with any child. It's never too late to start and no child is too far gone.

Our method is based on the belief that you are raising an adult. We believe in nurturing the individual to become the best version of themselves. We believe in giving kids the tools they need to manage themselves in the real world. If you're ready to leave the excuses behind and to lead by example, this is the book for you!

Introduction

To all sleep deprived parents: this is the book we've been promising. Follow our method fully; no shortcuts, no gadgets, no excuses, and your baby will sleep through the night,

Independent sleep is the direct result of conscious parenting. You decide if that is what you want. To raise an independent child, ideally starts at a young age. We are ambitious and committed, with a firm goal in mind, 12 hours of continuous night sleep, a 1-hour morning nap, and a 2-hour afternoon nap. There will be obstacles, especially during the first three years. Every developmental stage is an opportunity for your baby to grow and develop their skills, to become better sleepers. Therefore, it's important for parents to not just want a baby that can sleep well at night but an independent baby overall. There needs to be an understanding that crying is your baby's way of communicating. Once there is acceptance, that crying is a communication tool, you will begin to be able to differentiate between a need cry and a want cry.

Parents also need to take stock; your baby's habits did not happen overnight. They were built with patience and consistency. We know, you're probably side eyeing the book right now, but it's true. Every concession you made, every middle of the night feeding, every little thing you did to get your baby to sleep just five more minutes has led you to this point. Your baby has been trained. Now you weren't thinking long term when you made those concessions. We know they were made with the best intentions. We also know that we don't always make the best decisions at 3:00 am when we're exhausted. However, you must understand that your baby's bad habits didn't happen overnight. Learning takes time, patience, and practice. There is no way to speed up the learning process. Your baby will learn at their own pace. Be prepared to be that much more patient, because it will not happen on your ideal timing, your baby is developing from within. Embrace that this is a learning experience for both you and your child.

One of our main goals with this book, is to take all the societal pressures and expectations out of the equation. The amount of pressure put on parents is overwhelming. It's the easiest thing in the world to tell a parent to feed on demand, to wear their babies, to bounce on balls whistling lullabies while feeding, it's much harder to live those realities. Leave those judgements and societal/familial expectations at the door. At the end of the day, make decisions that work best for your family. No one else lives with the results of those choices. So, if your baby's needs are being met, they are healthy and developing at a good rate, that's all that matters. Your family being content, satisfied, and at peace should be what it's all about.

Our goal is to have your baby sleeping the optimum amount of time for their age and to do so independently. You will notice that if you start using our method at the beginning (12 weeks) you will be able to navigate illness, developmental stages, travelling, and all the challenges of life more easily because independence is a way of life. The fascinating part of sleep training is that progress and positive results are what will empower parents to hold on to their goals. All you need, is to be brave and take that first step.

Biology is on your side. As a species, humans sleep at night. Growth, regeneration, and memory retention all happen while we sleep. The first 24 months is the biggest developmental stage in a human life in terms of growth. Studies have repeatedly shown the importance of long periods of continuous uninterrupted sleep. Studies have also shown the importance of scheduled regular naps on memory retention and the importance sleep has in overall cognitive abilities and health.

Our method will give you the tools to help your baby develop these skills in a compassionate way. Although crying is going to be part of the process, we do not believe in letting babies cry endlessly. You will be an active part of this learning process and will learn just as much as your baby does. Our short-term goal is to get your baby sleeping through the night. Our long-term goal is to help you raise an independent sleeper, something that will benefit them their entire life.

This book was written with a busy parent in mind. It's not meant to be read cover to cover. Reading it in its entirety will certainly help you prepare for what's ahead and understand how you may have developed the habits you're looking to break. However, if you really don't have the time, rest assured. Take the time to read the introduction and the first chapter, since it will give you the basics of our method. After that, skip ahead to the chapter that is relevant to your baby's current age range. Inside that chapter you'll find everything you need to get your baby sleeping through the night. We address developmental phases that can affect sleep, common habits that have formed, and other important factors that are age specific. Three chapters is all it will take. Later, you can always refer back and find everything you need right where you expect it to be.

Let's get started.

The Babycoach Method 10 years later.

We expanded our methods and how it applies to older children. Throughout the last 10 years, many studies have emphasized how important scheduled extended amounts of sleep are. We have found that our method can be effectively applied to children as old as 7 years. Very few things have changed as far as our general approach. A few of the changes are due to the new guidelines regarding infant safety. Some changes, like the lovie, come due to increased exposure to older children.

Introduction

Lovie

Do not recommend before 6 months.

We've found that a small percentage of babies, between 4 and 6 months, can pull a flat blankie over their face, but do not quite can remove it at will. We've decided that having the baby in the crib without anything is best.

If, you as a parent, decide that the baby needs some comfort, we suggest the lovie (stuffed animal, toy, blankie) be no larger than baby's face (surface area) and small enough that they cannot lodge their face in it. Free flow of oxygen when your baby is in deep sleep is paramount.

Swaddle

We now recommend that parents, at the age of 8 weeks, start eliminating any swaddling they may be using with their newborn. We recommend only a loose swaddle from birth until 4 weeks. The sooner you expose your baby to the freedom needed to develop the muscles necessary to master the startle reflex, the easier it will be to fully eliminate the swaddle. This will make sleep training at 8 weeks more efficient and overall easier on your baby.

At week 8, you should begin to swaddle from the chest down, i.e. both arms free. At week 10, we encourage you to begin using footy pajamas. A sleep sack may be used if it allows for free range of motion. Eliminating the swaddle includes any magic suits that restrict movement or promise to help your baby sleep.

Pacifier

We now recommend that parents be a bit more conservative in using pacifiers. Using the pacifier for the nighttime routine is still very effective, to calm your baby while you bathe, change their clothing, hold the off for the feeding.

The rules for the pacifier are simple

Offer the pacifier three times within the first 30 minutes of placing a baby in their crib. After that (3 times or 30 minutes whichever comes first), the pacifier should be used only in the early hours of the morning, i.e. 11 hours after you placed your baby in the crib, to help them make it to the first feeding of the day. We have found that parents can become overly reliant on it throughout the process. Parents often find that they must go in many times overnight to offer the pacifier, which defeats the purpose of sleep training.

The pacifier can still be used liberally during the day, especially when you're establishing the four-hour feeding schedule. At night, we recommend using other self-soothing tools, patting, shushing, holding, etc. The pacifier can be reintroduced after your baby develops the ability to find it on their own and reinsert it at will. If you must help them, they are not ready to have it be reintroduced.

Introduction

If you're training a baby older than 6 months, you can still use the pacifier, as long as you're not the one putting it in your baby's mouth. You can have 10 pacifiers in their crib as far as we're concerned! However, if you must help them use it, we strongly recommend you eliminate it. You can make it available for their day routine.

Dream feeds

The purpose of a dream feed is to schedule a middle of the night feeding around what is convenient to you, the parent. The goal is to sneak in extra food in the hopes that baby will sleep longer. It is a habit you are instilling, that eventually you are going to have to break.

Introducing dream feeds never made sense to us. Whatever calories your baby consumes at night, they will be less motivated to consume during the day. These feedings just ensure that your baby will have a physical need to wake up the next night.

Breastfeeding and Sleep training

We've been approached by many women who mistakenly believed that sleep training is not an option while exclusively breastfeeding. It's important to first understand our position on breastfeeding. We believe breastfeeding is the optimal way to feed a baby.

Breastmilk is the perfect food, so for that reason alone, we will always recommend it.

That being said, we do feel that breastfeeding should only be used as a way to feed your baby. Too often, in the process of learning your baby's cues, cries, and needs, mothers find themselves being used as a soothing tool. An important part of the sleep training process, putting a feeding schedule in place, relies on breastfeeding mothers being able to start understanding their baby's different cries and being able to note when their baby is using breastfeeding for nourishment and when they're being used as a soothing tool.

It's important for us to emphasize that breastfeeding on demand, and really any on demand feeding, is the reason so many experience difficulties with our method, not breastfeeding itself. As long as parents understand this distinction (breastfeeding for food not soothing) and are fully committed to following the sleep training process, they will have the same success with our method.

Mothers who make the commitment to breastfeeding should understand that sleep is a primary need. Studies have proven that regular, scheduled periods of prolonged sleep have been shown to be as beneficial to a baby's long-term well-being as breastmilk has. Teaching your baby to independently sleep through the night is in no way a selfish decision. Having scheduled daytime feedings, is in no way a selfish decision. In fact, studies have shown that hungrier babies are more likely to fully empty their mother's breasts which leads to milk with a higher fat content. Babies who eat frequently throughout the day (on a one

Introduction

to two-hour schedule feeding) are less likely to fully empty their mother's breasts, which leads to milk with less fat, on average. Consider the fact that most babies will double their bodyweight by the time they're 16 to 20 weeks, and this becomes rather important.

Technology and sleep training

A flat, cleared crib and mattress combo is the ideal environment in which to train a baby. Unless your pediatrician recommends something for health reasons, a standard crib and mattress is all we recommend. There is no gadget that will make this process easier. Don't waste your money. We recommend pajamas and a sleep sack, no swaddles or sleep suits. Ultimately, anything that promises to help ease your baby to sleep or make them stay asleep will become a bad habit that will make sleep training more difficult.

Since our last book, the AAP has released new guidelines for parents regarding infant sleep.

Room sharing for the first 6 months

You can easily sleep train a baby while sleeping in the same room. Parents just have to be that much more disciplined in how you respond to your baby. You must temper your expectations; it will take a little longer. The early mornings (especially the last two hours of sleep) will be tougher to master for your baby and will require you to adjust your morning routine during the training process.

      We believe that everything that can make sleep training more challenging, is really an opportunity for your baby to become that much better. Don't shy away from challenges because they equal growth. Parents must adjust temporarily in order to make the process easier for the baby. The important word here is temporarily, we don't want you walking on eggshells forever.

Things to keep in mind while room sharing

    Lights

    Noises

    Alarms and technology

    Increased emotional impact

    Sleep deprivation

We strongly encourage parents to follow all safety guidelines whenever possible. We believe in safety first. Our method can work under any scenario.

Chapter One

The Four Babycoach Fundamentals of Sleep Training

There are four basic elements that should be used to sleep train your baby at any age after 12 weeks. You should also revert to these fundamentals if you ever feel that your baby's sleep is not where it should be.

We at Babycoach believe most babies fall into one of two categories: the sprinter, a baby that can cry very intensely but can only sustain it for a short period of time, or the endurance baby, a baby that won't cry as intensely but can maintain that low level of crying for a long period of time. Assess which category your baby falls into so that you can be somewhat prepared for what the training will bring.

The four basics of sleep training

Baby is healthy

Before you begin sleep training, take two to three days to assess your baby's overall behavior. If your baby is eating well, displaying their everyday demeanor, showing no signs of illness, showing no signs of teething (specifically a tooth that is about to break the gumline), etc. We do not recommend that you start training if your baby is about to or has just received vaccinations. If your baby has been diagnosed with any ailment, make sure your pediatrician is kept up to date throughout the process. Their medications should also be up to date and the ailment should be reasonably under control.

If, at any point in the training process your baby begins to show signs of illness, training should be stopped immediately and should resume when all signs of that illness have passed. When in doubt, suspend training for a couple of days until you're able to more clearly assess your baby's health. Remember that no baby is only sick at 2:00 am, if they're really coming down with an illness the signs will be present throughout their day. Pausing the training will allow

Chapter One

you to see if they are truly ill or if the issue is behavioral.

Baby is safe

We strongly recommend that babies sleep in their own crib. New guidelines from the AAP recommend that babies sleep in the same room as their parents until six months. If you choose to train, and baby is in their own nursery before six months, we strongly recommend using an Angel monitor or something similar, to monitor your baby's breathing during the overnight hours. If you are following the AAP guidelines and are room sharing, we do recommend babies still sleep in their own crib. We find that bassinets or baskets are too small and will restrict movement.

Within their cribs, we have the following recommendations. We find breathable net bumpers will prevent little feet from getting stuck between the rails. No loose blankets, a sleep sack is preferable since they allow for full range of motion but are secured by their own body weight. We recommend introducing a lovie only after six months, or when your baby has the dexterity to move the lovie at will, whichever comes last. Any soothing toys given before six months should be lightweight and small enough for your baby to move easily.

Ideally, your baby will have complete range of motion and the space to use that freedom to self soothe at will. If in doubt, always keep that in mind. Anything that can become a danger should be eliminated.

Baby is in an environment conducive to sleep

Ideally, your baby's sleep environment should be dark. Until they're eight months, the darker the better. After nine months, a nightlight can be used if needed. The nightlight should be placed behind a piece of furniture, hamper, etc. in a way that ensures that the light is diffused. We still want to stay away from direct sources of light. The nightlight should be dim enough to not stimulate your baby but should be bright enough to allow your baby to recognize their surroundings. The best way to assess is to take time, before you begin sleep training, to sit in their room in the middle of the night for 15 minutes. It will take about that long for your eyes to fully adjust. You want to put yourself in the same environment as your baby. See what they see. Cover any source of light in your baby's direct line of sight, this can include clocks, wiper warmers, humidifiers, etc. Hall lights should always be turned off. If needed, another nightlight can be added outside the room so that you can see.

The ideal temperature is between 65-72 degrees. Research has found that optimum restorative sleep occurs when sleeping in a slightly cooler environment. To assess if your baby is comfortable overnight you can

Chapter One

touch the tip of their nose or the tips of their ears. If they are cool to the touch, make a mental note to feel your baby's feet at the first diaper change. If they are also cool to the touch, you should raise the temperature slightly or add/modify their clothing layers, i.e. add socks, a long sleeve onesie instead of short sleeve, add a sleep sack, etc. If your baby's legs and feet are cool to the touch, use thicker fabrics as well as more layers. Their hands should not be used as a gauge since they will frequently be cooler to the touch due to the repeated exposure to moisture and air.

Your baby's mattress should be flat unless directed by your pediatrician or if they're younger than 12 weeks. Avoid contoured mattress inserts or wedges since they can inhibit your baby's ability to move freely.

The use of soothing sounds (waves, rain, running water) is recommended. White noise is great at masking ambient noise, but does not provide the emotional comfort that soothing sounds and or lullabies do. Natural noises are best until 6 months, instrumental lullabies from 6-12 months, and lullabies with lyrics for babies older than 12 months are ideal. Lullabies should be set to a slightly lower volume. We want to use the baby's natural curiosity in our favor. If the volume is slightly lower your baby will have to quiet themselves in order to be able to hear the lullabies, thus satisfying their curiosity. At the same time, a lower volume will help your baby stay calmer during their sleep cycles making it easier for them to fall back asleep without assistance or crying. Some parents believe that the volume should be loud enough to completely mask outside noises and to grab their baby's attention even while crying. Remember, if you raise a flexible baby, they will be able to perform well in all sorts of environments. Your baby will adjust to whatever noise level exists if they are gradually exposed to it.

Baby is in an emotional place where they can learn

Here is where all the sleep training happens. The first three basics are to ensure that your baby is in the best starting position possible. We believe sleep training is essentially giving your baby the opportunity to try to develop a skill they're innately equipped to develop. If the settings are right your baby, at their own pace, will figure out how to go to sleep, stay asleep, and wake up happy.

Our experience has shown that "bad" habits or sleep issues happen or were triggered by the parent's need to sleep. After weeks of interrupted sleep, it's not a surprise that parents start compromising, unknowingly creating the habits that will ultimately further disturb the family's ability to sleep. Before you are your baby's parent, you are a human being. Your needs are just as essential as your baby's. Sleep is a primary need; you need a certain amount of it to survive, to function. You can go longer without food than you can without sleep, it's that important. Lack of sleep will affect you emotionally, physically, and intellectually. Your baby will gain two-fold by learning how to sleep independently. A rested baby is a happier baby. They are easier to manage, readier to learn, and emotionally more even keeled. A rested parent is a better parent.

Chapter One

You will be rested enough to handle all of life's ups and down at your best.

Because this is a learning process, we do not believe in just letting your baby cry it out. We believe that your baby will reach a point where they are so frustrated that they are no longer learning. Crying is your baby's only method of communication, so some crying is inevitable. This process will help you develop the ability to understand what your baby is trying to communicate with their crying. A needy cry is different than a wanting cry.

Throughout this process you will establish that you are in charge. Baby will learn to follow your lead. Our approach will require discipline with compassion. For a baby to do what they're naturally equipped to do, parents must allow their baby room to grow. As much as they will learn, you will also have to learn to be comfortable taking a supporting role in this process. Meeting your baby's needs is crucial, but meeting their wants is not always in their best interest. Your job is to be patient enough to let them learn at their own pace.

Sleep training rules

Three-minute rule

Timer should start when your baby begins to cry intensely, think orange/red line on the monitor. If after three minutes your baby has maintained that intense level of crying and has shown no signs of trying to self soothe, you can enter their room and help them calm down. Time in their room must be limited to 3 minutes. After this three-minute reset, place your baby back in their crib and exit the room. This rule should be repeated as needed until your baby falls asleep. If during the three minutes your baby's cry diminishes for a minute, the timer should be restarted. This rule is best for babies 3-6 months.

Five-minute rule

This is basically the three-minute rule, but we consider your baby's increased ability to understand and willfully resist. Instead of monitoring them for a period of three minutes we give them 5 minutes. If after that time their crying does not diminish or they show no signs of trying to self soothe, you may enter their room for 3 minutes. This rule is best for babies 6 months and older

15-minute rule - Patience Practice

We apply this rule in the early morning and during the second half of a baby's naps during nap training. After your baby has slept 11 hours it is more difficult for them to fall back to sleep. At this point, everything that was working in their favor at bedtime is now working against them; your baby is pretty well rested, they're getting hungry, the sun is coming up, their diaper is wet, etc. Our goal when using this rule is to eliminate the expectation your baby may develop that someone will come rushing in once they've woken up.

Chapter One

Once your baby starts fussing after the 11 hours, you can set your timer. Your baby does not have to reach an intense level of crying. Once they go from a happy talking sound to a whinier cry or whimpering you can start your timer. Give them 15 minutes. After that you can go in and assess the situation. Again, you want to limit your time in the room to three minutes. Ideally you will go through two rounds of patience practice before picking your baby up for the day. The more your baby practices the more likely they will be to fall back to sleep during this time. You should notice that the intensity of your baby's cry should diminish with practice. You should also notice that the time they spend happily talking will increase. Every day you should try to get closer to your baby's scheduled wake up time.

When used during naps, the intensity of your baby's cry will depend on how well your baby's nap has gone. There is a chance that your baby may cry intensely for 15-minute increments before they fully master the second half of the nap. We strongly recommend that you start nap training only when your baby is able to fully sleep through the night for at least 7 consecutive nights. If, for any reason, your baby is finding it especially difficult to master the 11th hour of sleep, consider beginning nap training anyway. The extra practice during the morning nap may be what they need to get over that hump.

Chapter Two

Three to Six Months

If your baby has been previously trained with our method, go back to the four fundamentals and begin implementing them. At this age, reverting to the basics and that "training mentality" will get your baby back sleeping through the night quickly. For example, one learns how to walk. Fast forward 20 years and you twist your ankle. You haven't forgotten how to walk. With a little rehab, you will walk the exact way you always have. Same principle applies here. Once your baby knows how to sleep through the night and the skills associated with it, they'll never forget. Because sleep is a primary need, it's very easy to get caught trying to justify why a baby is waking up. Creating short term solutions will eventually hinder your baby's ability to sleep independently but won't erase the skills they've already learned.

If your baby has not been trained before or has been trained using another method (especially the cry it out method) then following the four basics of sleep training will teach your baby how to fall asleep independently, how to self soothe throughout the night, and how to wake up happy after sleeping 12 hours.

Before you begin training parents must make an honest assessment of their starting point and the issues they're facing. Parents must understand that your baby has ingrained habits that will make the training process a bit more challenging. Be ready for the rigors of the training process. At this point, it's more about the parent's ability to respond consistently and be patient enough to stick with it. It's important to acknowledge your role in whatever patterns or habits that have been developed and are now a hurdle. Every baby is a unique individual that will learn at their own pace. While the first two to three nights of training will be difficult, you can expect to see positive results more quickly at this stage. Compared to sleep training a baby under 12 weeks, the amount of crying may be elevated but results come much more quickly.

Chapter Two

How to sleep train at this age

Baby is healthy

By now your baby has stabilized. The first 12 weeks your baby had to adjust to a new environment. The baby went from a perfect environment, where everything was balanced, to a not so perfect environment where they had to learn how to process food, regulate temperature, process lights/sounds, etc. The primary concern to sleep training during the first 12 weeks is growth and making sure that your baby is consuming enough calories. That is less of a concern between 3-6 months, ideally your baby will be already on a basic set routine, if not refer to our book The Baby Sleep Solution or 12 Hours by 12 Weeks Old.

At this point your baby will be starting solids, so they should be able to easily consume enough food to continue growing at a good rate. Dropping any nighttime feedings should occur at a faster pace. Parents try to encourage feedings during the day in the hopes that the baby will sleep longer at night. You will increase those odds by eliminating the night feedings. It is only by decreasing the night feedings that your baby will begin to consume more during the day.

The total amount your baby eats should be somewhere between 30-36 ounces of food per day. Once they reach this limit, which usually occurs around 5 months, most pediatricians will begin to recommend adding solids into your baby's diet. When you begin introducing solids, the total amount of ounces or minutes from nursing will tend to decrease. This is the point where solids slowly start becoming their primary source of calories. Your baby will be satisfied enough to sleep through the night.

It's also important to point out, that it's the total amount of ounces during the day, that will enable your baby to sleep through the night. Parents often get hung up on their baby's last bottle, don't. If they've eaten enough during their other three feedings, they should be just fine.

As far as teething, if your baby has an average day, feeding well and showing no signs of pain/discomfort, it is okay to begin training. Our experience has shown that the most painful and disruptive teeth are the front two upper and lower teeth, they often get in the way of sleep training. After the gums have been broken by a tooth, the ones that follow are much less eventful. On average, it becomes easier and less disruptive to your baby's routine.

Baby is safe

Your baby should be on a flat mattress, with secure fitted sheets. We suggest using the Angel monitor at this point if you are not room sharing. It will make the transition to sleeping in a separate room easier on parents. Breathable net bumpers may be used, especially if your baby tends to get their arms or legs caught in the crib slats. We recommend removing any mobiles or in crib toys.

To parents following the AAP guidelines and room sharing we suggest many of the same precautions. Baby should sleep in their own crib on a flat mattress with secure fitted sheets. We do not recommend smaller sleep environments, i.e. bassinets, baskets, or half cribs since they may prevent babies from moving freely throughout the night.

Baby is in an environment conducive to sleep

Before you begin training, we recommend that you spend 10-15 minutes in your baby's nursery in the middle of the night. This will allow you to see what your baby will see if they do wake up, during the night. Any sources of direct light should be covered. You will notice that ambient light will seep through blinds, under the door. That's why these 10-15 minutes of assessment is so important, it will allow your eyes to adjust.

New guidelines suggest that your baby's nursery should be between 65- and 72-degrees Fahrenheit. A cooler environment is more conducive to sleep. During seasonal changes, parents should be especially conscious of overnight temperatures since they can affect internal room temperature and humidity.

As for sounds, at this point, your baby will benefit most from a repetitive natural sound. Ocean waves, rainfall, thunderstorms, etc. can all be used. We do not recommend white noise since it only serves to mask outside sounds but does not provide the emotional comfort natural sounds do.

Baby is in an emotional place where they can learn

When training begins trust your knowledge of your baby. We always suggest that parents consider starting on a Friday so that the most difficult nights occur when they don't have work or other considerations. This also frees parents to work together so that they may take turns during the overnight hours. Remember, sleep is a primary need, you need sleep too!

Establishing a nighttime routine is essential to the overall process. It will physically signal to your baby that it's time to slow down and ease them into a more restful mood. Your nighttime routine can include bathing (not necessarily done every night), changing them into pajamas, reading 2-3 short books (soft light should be used if possible), singing songs, anything that you really enjoy doing that is not overly stimulating. Remember though, that consistency is key. Choose activities that you wouldn't mind doing frequently. The final step in your nighttime routine should be the final feeding so plan accordingly.

Once you've gone through the nighttime routine, they should be put in the crib awake. Lights should then be turned off and parents should exit the nursery. It's very important that you put your baby in their crib

Chapter Two

awake if and when possible. The beginning of the night is the best time for you to introduce changes. If your baby is asleep before you place them in their crib, they will miss the opportunity to develop the skills necessary for them to fall back asleep independently in the middle of the night. Be aware, the first time you try putting your baby down awake, and they have not had the opportunity to fall asleep without assistance, it will take them, on average, 45 minutes to 90 minutes for them to fall asleep independently. Depending on how old your baby is, you may not be able to practice every night. As your baby grows, this will become easier to do especially towards six months. As always, do the best you can today and try again tomorrow.

Once you place them in their crib, begin using the three-minute rule. Wait to start the timer until their cry reaches an intense level. The monitor sound indicator line should be between orange and red. If after three minutes they've maintained this intense level of crying and have shown no signs of trying to self soothe, you can go in for three minutes. The purpose of you going in is twofold, first to fix whatever your baby can not fix themselves, i.e. dirty diaper, light left on, stuck in odd position, etc., second to help calm your baby from a place where they're too emotional back down to a level where you can see that they've gotten ahold of themselves.

For the first minute, try to help your baby calm down by shushing, softly speaking short concise directions "go night-night" or "it's all right, I love you". If after a minute, these techniques have not managed to calm your baby, it is okay to pick your baby up for the remaining two minutes. Hold your baby tight, like you would a hysterical adult. We don't recommend rocking or pacing. Holding your baby is about human contact and providing emotional reassurance.

After the three minutes are done, put your baby back in their crib and walk out of the room. Repeat, repeat, repeat. The first 20 minutes of your baby's night will almost certainly be intense. It may feel like you going in makes things worse. That's normal. It is important, that you do so, because that is what will break the pattern of behavior that has been created before now. Your baby is under the assumption that the louder they cry the faster you'll respond. Don't be surprised if your baby wails louder and moves around in protest when you first enter their nursery and when you place them back in their crib. At the three-minute mark, you must place your baby back in their crib even if they are still crying.

It's important to keep in mind that the three-minute reset is as much for you as it is for your baby. This is a highly emotional process and the time spent reassuring your baby is also time for you to collect yourself. While you're out of the room, monitoring, take the time to calm yourself. We cannot overstate how emotional this can be on a parent, so make sure to take your feelings into account. Your baby can feel your stress. Take the three minutes to center yourself and to calm as much as possible so that your baby can sense your confidence when you do enter the room.

Usually after 20 minutes, you will notice that your baby will start making better use of the time you're spending out of their room. This is where you will really begin to see signs of self-soothing. If, at any point, your baby shows signs of calming, crying slows for longer than 60 seconds or they begin to try to physically self soothe, i.e. roll, suck on their hands, or try to find the pacifier, reset the timer. If you're at all unsure if you should go in, add another minute to the timer. You don't want to go in just before your baby has the aha moment.

Write down everything during this process, when they wake up, how long they cry, how intense, etc. This will help you see progress. Once your baby falls asleep, the consecutive wake ups will be less intense and will not last as long. The average time of a middle of the night wake up is usually between 15 to 20 minutes. This is the case until the 11th hour.

In the first three days of training, after the 11th hour, depending on how upset your baby is, its ok to stop the training at this hour. Again, this only applies for the first few days of training. We don't want to overwhelm your baby or you so this is a temporary allowance that we make in order to keep you motivated. There are three things we are trying to teach your baby: how to go to sleep, how to stay asleep, and how to wake up happy. How to wake up happy is the last step of the training. It is where we address the 11th hour. Early wake ups are the most challenging part of the sleep training process. This is why it is so beneficial to long term sleep skills. This 11th hour will also help with the nap training, since this hour most closely resembles their naps.

After the three days of training, you should see enough progress during the night, to start applying the 15-minute rule, to that 11th hour. Your baby by now should be having long stretches of restorative sleep, she will wake up somewhat rested and happy. Don't rush in, the main purpose of the 15-minute rule is to give your baby a chance to learn patience. From the moment your baby stops "talking" and starts whimpering (does not have to be full on crying) where you see that they're beginning to escalate, start your timer. After 15 minutes, go in. You have three minutes to assess the situation and help them calm slightly. After the three minutes, leave the room. Do another round of 15 minutes.

If they're still crying after two round of patience practice, you can go in and start their day. Ideally, they would maintain their scheduled feeding. Do your best to hold them off. We suggest at least one round of the 15-minute rule. Two rounds of 15-minute "patience practice" are ideal. Let the intensity of the crying and your baby's mood determine how many rounds of 15-minute practice you'll do.

When you do decide to start their day, turn on the lights, open the blinds, and start talking to your baby in a happy voice, i.e. "Good morning! What's all this fuss about? You did such a great job!". We want your baby to calm slightly before you pick them up. Show them with nonverbal communication that everything is ok. At this age, their first reaction will be an increase in their crying because they think you're going to leave again. By waiting until your baby calms slightly, you will teach them they do not need to cry in order to get picked up. They will start to connect that this morning routine means their day is starting and in time they will smile when you come in. We want to start rewarding positive behaviors.

Chapter Two

Things you should expect during this age range, that may disrupt sleeping.

Four Month Sleep "Regression"

Around 16 weeks, your baby begins to understand cause and effect, i.e. if they cry, they get a response, if they cry harder the response comes faster. Your baby starts to understand how to communicate their wants and needs. All their needs must be met, but not necessarily their wants. You should, by now, know your baby well enough to understand the difference.

Raising an independent sleeper takes time, resolve, and consistent effort. This is especially true if your baby has developed habits, which, let's face it, is all too easy to do during their first 16 weeks. Between illnesses, reflux, colic, and sleep deprivation on your part, things happen. That's why we don't refer to this developmental stage as a regression, but rather a progression. If you haven't had the opportunity to sleep train your baby and teach them independent sleep skills, increasingly frequent wake ups are a natural part of this developmental phase.

Rolling

Your baby will learn to roll to their side, to their belly, and then from their belly to their front. This will result in more frequent wake ups in the middle of the night. We encourage you to sleep train your baby by putting them to sleep on their backs. Chances are, that is your baby's least favorite position, but it is the safest. Tummy sleep is usually a baby's preferred position.

Once they can flip themselves, we encourage you to be proactive during the day to make nights safer. Lots of tummy and back time will help your baby develop the muscles and the ability to flip themselves back and forth at will. Extra practice will also lead to greater efficiency. You cannot stop development or slow it down. Once your baby learns to roll, they'll only start to do it more often.

If you find yourself worried or wanting to flip your baby in the middle of the night, let that be your reminder to work more throughout the day. Five to ten-minute windows of practice, ideally three to five times a day. Once baby is skilled on rolling back and forth, we encourage you to stop flipping them in the middle of the night.

Teething

In our experience, we find that teething should not be that disruptive to sleep training. It's an annoyance more than anything. Increased drooling, gum irritation and redness, increased rooting and chewing are all clear signs of teething. We find that the extensive drooling happens mostly when the two upper and two lower front teeth are coming in. Drooling will decrease as your baby's tongue, jaw, and cheek muscles develop which mainly occurs once solids are introduced. Pain will only happen when the tooth is breaking through the gum line. This pain will decrease as more teeth come in.

If in doubt, check on your baby. You're looking for a feverish temperature, loose stool, redness, swelling, etc. We always believe in the middle of the night, if you're in doubt, suspend training until the next day. Finish the night the best way you can. Observe your baby during the next day or two, if the tooth is about to break through, they will still be irritable and cranky. If the tooth is about to break the gum line, you can suspend training until the tooth emerges or they start to feel better.

If your baby is happy and eating normally during the day, remember that pain does not happen only at 2:00 am. If your baby is acting normally after a "teething" scare in the middle of the night, teething was not the issue, restart the training that night. Being proactive during the day will always make the nights easier to handle.

Introducing Solid foods and how that may affect sleep

Because solid food is a natural progression in your baby's development, we do recommend parents introduce solids on schedule. Solid foods are not only nutritionally important but physically important as well. The exercise with the spoon will help your baby with speech, development of teeth, and motor coordination. Speak to your pediatrician about when you should begin introducing solids. Often, we see pediatricians begin recommending solids around six months, but it can occur as early as four.

When you begin, we suggest offering the new food during the second feeding. This will give your baby time enough to process the food and time enough for you to notice any possible adverse reactions. Parents should introduce the new feedings at "lunch" before bottle or breastfeeding.

As the number of solid feedings increases you will notice that the amount they eat from the bottle or breast will decrease, that is very natural. All new foods should always be introduced at the lunchtime or second feeding. We recommend giving the same food at least 3-4 times before trying something new. This will give your baby a chance to adjust to the new flavor and texture before you decide if they like it or not. This also allows you to see any reactions your baby may have to a food while minimizing any possible confusion. Once your baby has adjusted to the new food and is ready for a second meal, you can begin giving that food at their first feeding, breakfast.

The last solid meal to be introduced should be dinner. Let the last solid feeding be 90 minutes before bedtime to give your baby a chance to partially digest the food and be hungry enough for a bottle at bedtime. This will also give you the opportunity to break up your nighttime routine without feeling overly rushed due to the messiness of solid feedings.

Chapter Two

Introducing First Solid Feeding
7:00 AM to 7:00 PM Schedule

7:00 AM – Wake up. First feeding

11:00 AM – Second feeding. Solids followed by breastfeeding or formula

3:00 PM – Third Feeding

6:30 PM – Fourth Feeding

Introducing Second Solid Feeding
7:00 AM to 7:00 PM Schedule

7:00 AM – Wake up. First feeding. Breastfeeding or formula followed by solids.

11:00 AM – Second feeding. Solids followed by breastfeeding or formula

3:00 PM – Third feeding

6:30 PM – Fourth feeding

Do not start sleep training the day you introduce a new food. Schedule up to three days/nights where you're certain your baby's schedule will be the same. On the nights you introduce a new food, make sure that you go in to check on your baby if they cry or wake more frequently than usual. Change the diaper if they have soiled it. Try to do it in the crib. If you are unable to, try to minimize any stimulation your baby may receive and put them back in their crib as quickly as possible. Remember that solids are often more difficult to digest and more calorie dense. If you notice that you baby "isn't eating as much" don't automatically assume that they're hungry at night.

Introducing Third Solid Feeding Schedule

7:00 AM to 7:00 PM Schedule

7:00 AM – First feeding. Breastfeeding or formula followed by solids.

11:00 AM – Second feeding. Solids followed by breastfeeding or bottle.

3:00 PM – Third feeding

5:30 – Dinner feeding. Solids only

6:30 PM – Fourth feeding. Breastfeeding or formula only.

Chapter Two

Babycoach case study

Bella was solely breastfed and had a habit of falling asleep while feeding. She would wake two to three times overnight to nurse in order to fall back asleep. When Bella developed the ability to roll, her nighttime sleep deteriorated. She began to wake seven to eight times a night and nursing slowly became less effective.

The increased number of nighttime feedings also affected her daytime feedings. Due to the increase in calories consumed at night, she became very unmotivated to eat during her scheduled feedings.

How we sleep trained Bella

First, we instructed her mother to reinstitute the four-hour feeding schedule during Bella's day. This meant that Bella needed to be woken up from an unscheduled nap in order to eat. Feedings could occur as soon as three hours if she was especially fussy, but our overall goal was four hours between feedings. We encouraged her parents to begin keeping a thorough log to track her progress and allow us to see any patterns in behavior that would emerge with the training process. Putting the set daytime feeding schedule in place was the focus of the first two days of training.

We instructed Bella's parents to continue this three/four-hour schedule during the overnight hours as well. This helped to eliminate feedings that were occurring too frequently. The only difference was that, at night, they weren't to wake Bella if she slept longer than four hours.

While this was happening, we encouraged Bella's parents to do lots of tummy time to help her develop the muscles and coordination necessary to roll more efficiently. Since this is a natural developmental progression, we wanted to focus on enabling Bella and not trying to restrict or prevent rolling.

Once the daytime feeding schedule was in place for two days, we started to focus on eliminating the remaining nighttime feedings. Since Bella was eating very well during the day, we decided to eliminate all the feedings together. We had Bella's mom pump during the day in order to give Bella breastmilk at night. This gave Bella a chance to practice bottle feeding. An added benefit is that it also helped Bella's mom to start establishing her own rhythm of pumping before bed in order to get more sleep before needing to pump again.

Due to Bella's age, we decided to eliminate an ounce per feeding per night. We worked with Bella after feedings to help her fall back to sleep and helped her stay calm until her next scheduled feeding four hours later. It took us three nights to fully eliminate all the nighttime feedings.

Bella was still waking up so we began to use the three-minute rule to help Bella develop her own self soothing skills. We began to consistently reinforce the three-minute rule for the first eleven hours of sleep. After the first three nights of using the three-minute rule we also began to use the 15-minute patience

Chapter Two

practice rule during the last hour of sleep. This gave Bella more opportunities to practice since she had begun to sleep more and self sooth more efficiently by that point.

Bella's parents took over at that point. They reinforced the three- and fifteen-minute rules for the two-week reinforcement period. After that they began nap training in order to continue challenging Bella's skills.

Chapter Three

Six to Nine Months

If your baby has been previously trained with our method, go back to the four fundamentals and begin implementing them. Depending on how long they've been struggling to sleep, on average they should be able to bounce back within five to seven nights.

If your baby has not been trained before or has been trained using another method, especially the cry it out method, begin training by making an honest assessment of your starting point and the issues you're facing. By now your baby has ingrained habits that will make the training process more challenging. Be ready for the rigors of the training process. At this point, it's more about your ability to respond consistently and be patient enough to stick with it. It's important to acknowledge your role in whatever patterns or habits that have been developed and are now a hurdle. Every baby is a unique individual that will learn at their own pace. While the first two to three nights of training will be difficult, parents should expect to see positive results more quickly at this stage.

How to sleep train at this age

Baby is healthy

At this point your baby will be starting solids if they haven't already. This means they should be able to easily consume enough food to continue growing at a good rate. Dropping any nighttime feedings should occur at a faster pace. Parents try to encourage feedings during the day in the hopes that the baby will sleep longer at night. You will increase those odds by eliminating the night feedings. It is only by decreasing the night feedings that your baby will begin to consume more during the day.

The total amount your baby eats should be somewhere between 30-36 ounces of food per day. Once they reach this limit, which usually occurs around 5 months, most pediatricians will begin to recommend adding solids into your baby's diet. When you begin introducing solids, the total amount of ounces or minutes from nursing will tend to decrease. Solids will slowly become their primary source of calories. Your baby will be satisfied enough to sleep through the night.

It's the total amount food consumed during the day, that enables your baby to sleep through the night. Parents often get hung up on their baby's last bottle, don't. If they've eaten enough during their other three feedings, they should be just fine.

Introducing First Solid Feeding

7:00 AM to 7:00 PM Schedule

7:00 AM – Wake up. First feeding

11:00 AM – Second feeding. Solids followed by breastfeeding or formula

3:00 PM – Third Feeding

6:30 PM – Fourth Feeding

Introducing Second Solid Feeding

7:00 AM to 7:00 PM Schedule

7:00 AM – Wake up. First feeding. Breastfeeding or formula followed by solids.

11:00 AM – Second feeding. Solids followed by breastfeeding or formula

3:00 PM – Third feeding

6:30 PM – Fourth feeding

Chapter Three

Introducing Third Solid Feeding Schedule

7:00 AM to 7:00 PM Schedule

7:00 AM – First feeding. Breastfeeding or formula followed by solids.

11:00 AM – Second feeding. Solids followed by breastfeeding or bottle.

3:00 PM – Third feeding

5:30 – Dinner feeding. Solids only

6:30 PM – Fourth feeding. Breastfeeding or formula only.

Baby is healthy, continued...

As far as teething, if your baby has an average day, feeding well and showing no signs of pain/discomfort, it is okay to begin training. Our experience has shown that the most painful and disruptive teeth are the front two upper and lower teeth, they often get in the way of sleep training. After the gums have been broken by a tooth, the ones that follow are much less eventful. Although every baby is different, on average, it becomes easier and less disruptive to your baby's routine.

Baby is safe

At this age, babies can safely begin to sleep in their own rooms. We suggest using the Angel monitor which will help monitor your baby's breathing during the night. It will make the transition to sleeping in a separate room easier if you previously room shared.

Your baby should be on a flat mattress, with secure fitted sheets. Breathable net bumpers may be used, especially if your baby tends to get their arms or legs caught in the crib slats. We recommend removing any mobiles or in crib toys. We do not recommend smaller sleep environments, i.e. bassinets, baskets, or half cribs since they may prevent babies from moving freely throughout the night.

Chapter Three

Baby is in an environment conducive to sleep

Before you begin training, we recommend that you spend 10-15 minutes in your baby's nursery sometime after your baby falls asleep. This will allow you to see what your baby sees if they do wake up, during the night. Any sources of direct light should be covered. Ambient light will seep through blinds and under the door. That's why these 10-15 minutes of assessment are so important, it will allow your eyes to adjust.

New guidelines suggest that your baby's nursery should be between 65- and 72-degrees Fahrenheit. A cooler environment is more conducive to sleep. During seasonal changes, parents should be especially conscious of overnight temperatures since they can affect internal room temperature and humidity.

As for sounds, at this point, your baby will benefit most from instrumental lullabies. You may still use natural sounds if you prefer. In our experience, instrumental lullabies seem to be slightly more effective at helping babies to self soothe. We do not recommend white noise since it only serves to mask outside sounds but does not provide the emotional comfort natural sounds do.

Baby is in an emotional place where they can learn

When training begins trust your knowledge of your baby. We always suggest that parents consider starting on a Friday so that the most difficult nights occur when they don't have work or other considerations. This also frees parents to work together so that they may take turns during the overnight hours. Remember, sleep is a primary need, you need sleep too!

Establishing a nighttime routine is essential to the overall process. It will physically signal to your baby that it's time to slow down and ease them into a more restful mood. Your nighttime routine can include bathing (not necessarily done every night), changing them into pajamas, reading 2-3 short books (soft light should be used if possible), singing songs, anything that you really enjoy doing that is not overly stimulating. Remember though, that consistency is key. Choose activities that you wouldn't mind doing frequently. The final step in your nighttime routine should be the final feeding so plan accordingly.

Once you've gone through the nighttime routine, they should be put in the crib awake. Lights should then be turned off and parents should exit the nursery. It's very important that you put your baby in their crib awake if and when possible. The beginning of the night is the best time for you to introduce changes. If your baby is asleep before you place them in their crib, they will miss the opportunity to develop the skills necessary for them to fall back asleep independently in the middle of the night. As always, do the best you can today and try again tomorrow. Be aware, the first time you try putting your baby down awake, and they have not had the opportunity to fall asleep without assistance, it will take them, on average, 45 minutes to 90 minutes for them to fall asleep independently.

Once you place them in their crib, begin using the five-minute rule. Wait to start the timer until their cry reaches an intense level (the monitor line should be between orange and red). If after five minutes they've maintained this intense level of crying and have shown no signs of trying to self soothe, you can go in for three minutes. The purpose of you going in is twofold, first to fix whatever your baby can not fix themselves (dirty diaper, light turned on, stuck in odd position), second to help calm your baby from a place where they're too emotional, down to a level where you can see that they've gotten ahold of themselves. For the first minute, try to help your baby calm down by shushing, softly speaking short concise directions "go night-night" or "it's all right, I love you". If after a minute, these techniques have not managed to calm your baby, it is okay to pick your baby up for the remaining two minutes. Hold your baby tight, like you would a hysterical adult. We don't recommend rocking or pacing. Holding your baby is about human contact and providing emotional reassurance. After the three minutes are done, put your baby back in their crib and walk out of the room. Repeat, repeat, repeat.

The first 20 minutes of your baby's night will almost certainly be intense. It may feel like you going in just makes things worse. That's normal. It is important, that you do so, because that is what will break the pattern of behavior that has been created before now. Your baby is under the assumption that the louder they cry the faster you'll respond. Don't be surprised if your baby wails louder and moves around in protest when you first enter their nursery and when you place them back in their crib. At the three-minute mark, you must place your baby back in their crib even if they are still crying.

It's important to keep in mind that the 3-minute reset is as much for you as it is for your baby. This is a highly emotional process and the time spent reassuring your baby is also time for you to reassure yourself. While you're out of the room, monitoring, take the time to calm yourself. We cannot overstate how emotional this can be on a parent, so make sure to take your feelings into account. Your baby can feel your stress. Take the five minutes to center yourself and to calm as much as possible so that your baby can sense your confidence when you do enter the room.

Usually after 20 minutes, you will notice that your baby will start making better use of the five minutes. This is where you will really begin to see signs of self-soothing. If, at any point, your baby shows signs of calming, crying slows for longer than 60 seconds or they begin to try to physically self soothe (roll, suck on their hands, or try to find the pacifier) reset the timer. If you're at all unsure if you should go in, add another minute to the timer. You don't want to go in just before your baby has the aha moment.

Write down everything during this process, when they wake up, how long they cry, how intense, etc. This will help you see progress. Once your baby falls asleep, the consecutive wake ups will be less intense and will not last as long. The average time of a middle of the

Chapter Three

night wake up is usually between 15 to 20 minutes. This is the case until the 11th hour.

The first night will be your baseline and will help you measure your baby's progress. The five-minute rule should be used until the 11th hour. At that point you will want to begin using the 15-minute rule. Ideally you will do at least two rounds of the 15-minute rule before beginning your baby's day. Their scheduled feeding time shouldn't change if you decide to pick them up early.

You should see significant improvement nightly as your baby practices. If the first night of training is fairly easy, prepare yourself for the second night, this is supposed to be challenging. By this age your baby should understand that change is happening. If the first night is easy the second night will often be more difficult because of this understanding. The third night is where you should start to see definitive improvement.

In the first three days of training, after the 11th hour, depending on how upset your baby is, its ok to stop the training at this hour. Again, this only applies for the first few days of training. We don't want to overwhelm your baby or you so this is a temporary allowance that we make in order to keep you motivated. There are three things we are trying to teach your baby: how to go to sleep, how to stay asleep, and how to wake up happy. How to wake up happy is the last step of the training. It is where we address the 11th hour. Early wake ups are the most challenging part of the sleep training process. This is why it is so beneficial to long term sleep skills. This 11th hour will also help with the nap training, since this hour most closely resembles their naps.

After the three days of training, you should see enough progress during the night, to start applying the 15-minute rule, to that 11th hour. Your baby by now should be having long stretches of restorative sleep, she will wake up somewhat rested and happy. Don't rush in, the main purpose of the 15-minute rule is to give your baby a chance to learn patience. From the moment your baby stops "talking" and starts whimpering (does not have to be full on crying) where you see that they're beginning to escalate, start your timer. After 15 minutes, go in. You have three minutes to assess the situation and help them calm slightly. After the three minutes, leave the room. Do another round of 15 minutes. If they're still crying, you can go in and start their day. Maintain their scheduled feeding, picking them up a little early is an exception but the feeding time is the rule. We suggest at least one round of the 15-minute rule. Two rounds of 15-minute "patience practice" are ideal. Let the intensity of the crying and your baby's mood determine how many rounds of 15-minute practice you'll do.

When you do decide to start their day, turn on the lights, open the blinds, and start talking to your baby in a happy voice, i.e. "Good morning! What's all this fuss about? You did such a great job!". We want your baby to calm slightly before you pick them up. Show them with nonverbal communication that everything is ok. At this age, their first reaction will be an increase in their crying because they think you're going to leave again. By waiting until your baby calms slightly, you will teach them they do not need to cry in order to get picked up. They will start to connect that this morning routine means their day is starting and in time they will smile when you come in. We want to start rewarding positive behaviors.

Things you can expect during this developmental phase

Stranger anxiety (9 months)

Babies that are happy interacting with a trusted and known person, may suddenly start havening anxiety around people they don't interact often or strangers. The closer you get to 9 months the more evident this behavior will become. The more you cater to this discomfort, the shyer and more resistant your baby will become.

If you're starting the training process around the 8-month mark, you will notice these intense crying fits for their mother or primary caregiver. This is where it would be helpful for the other parent to take the lead. This is just a developmental stage, try not to cater to it.

Sitting up in crib

Sometime in this stage your baby will learn to sit upright on their own. Going from a seated position to a prone/supine position is a skill. Parents tend to place their baby laying down in their crib. You may find yourself, where your baby is sitting down crying and falls asleep sitting up, having refused to lay down. It's up to your baby to figure out how to go from sitting down to laying down. When you first begin training you can try to coax them into laying down, by gently patting on their side or guiding them to a laying position. Your baby will have to decide to lay themselves down. That will be the real breakthrough.

Throwing objects in anger to gain attention

You may find that once standing, your baby begins to throw things out of their crib, often their pacifier or lovie. This will cause their crying to increase. We recommend that the first three times this happens you place the item back into their crib. If they continue to throw the item out of the crib, then we recommend that you leave them where they are or remove them from the room for the night. We do not want your baby to learn that throwing the toy will get your attention. If they throw the toy, we want them to learn that eventually, they will have to go without it.

Actively seek adult attention

Because babies actively want to engage with adults you may find that their crying spikes when you enter their room. That is just your baby demanding what they have become accustomed to. Use the five-minute rule consistently.

The three minutes in the room becomes even more important at this age. You may see your baby to start crying more intensely when you place them back in their crib. Remember, crying is a communication tool.

Chapter Three

You leaving the room will send a very powerful message that crying will not yield the old reward.

Sleep training will be an opportunity to teach your baby new communication skills, which will result in less crying necessary to gain positive attention. You will notice a calmer and less demanding baby during the day because you did not reward the demand/respond pattern. Your baby will benefit two-fold with this practice. They will be generally calmer, and they will have a less stressed caregiver.

At this age they also, try to demand to be picked up and held more often, and assert their wants in a more willful way. What you encourage will remain. Make sure to give the attention the situation requires but try not to cater to these demands.

7:00 AM – 7:00 PM Schedule

Six to Nine Months

7:00 – 7:15 AM – Wake up

7:00 – 7:30 AM – First feeding

7:30 – 9:00 AM – Activity time

9:00 – 10:30 AM – Morning nap

10:30 – 11:00 AM – Activity time

11:00 – 11:30 AM – Second feeding

11:30 – 1:00 PM – Activity time

1:00 – 3:00 PM – Afternoon nap

3:00 – 3:30 PM – Third feeding

3:30 – 6:30 PM – Activity time

6:30 – 7:00 PM – Fourth feeding

7:00 PM – Bedtime

Chapter Three

Babycoach Case Study

Russell was 7 months and although he had slept fairly well on and off, his sleep was really impacted by teething. He was especially irritable at night. His parents found themselves rocking and walking around for increasingly longer amounts of time. They tried feeding as a way to console him as he started to wake up more frequently. Most nights he ended up in his parents' bed. He started to refuse his feedings during day, which increased their confusion, leading to more feedings at night as hunger became a concern.

How we trained Russell

We first addressed his teething. Although teething can be challenging, experience has shown us that it can be painful when it cuts through the gums on the first lower and upper teeth. Drooling usually goes away after that happens. Once we explained that to the parents, we assessed Russel's day behavior and decided we could move ahead with the training.

Because of his age we knew eliminating any feedings at night was the most urgent thing to do. They were not just having a negative impact on his caloric intake during the day, it was creating the habit of eating at night. We substantially cut the ounces of every feeding, using the three-minute rule in between the feedings. We gave him three nights to shift his eating habits.

Once that was in place, we allowed him two nights of practice without any feedings using the five-minute rule from 7:00 PM, his bed time, until 6:00 AM, his 11th hour. After 6:00 AM we used the 15 minutes Patience Practice rule until his scheduled wake up.

It took five nights for Russell to begin sleeping through the night. We instructed the parents to follow that plan for a two-week reinforcement period to cement his progress. After the reinforcement period, Russell began nap training.

Chapter Four

Nine to Twelve Months

If you have previously sleep trained your baby, you should go back to the four basics and begin to use them consistently again. One thing that parents should keep in mind is that by this age most babies have developed the ability to sit upright and will begin to show signs of trying to stand up. This can cause disruptions in nighttime sleep in otherwise great sleepers.

If you are training your baby for the first time you must understand, your baby has grown accustomed to a certain pattern of behavior that has been their normal. Breaking those habits will take a lot of discipline and resolve on your part. There will be a level of crying that can at times be very intense. Knowing your baby's personality, every parent should, by now, know what to expect as far as their crying goes. You will find that the first 20-30 minutes of training will be highly emotional and intense when it comes to crying as your baby realizes that what has otherwise worked for the last 9-12 months is no longer working.

How to sleep train at this age

Baby is healthy

At this point your baby is accustomed to solids and should be eating three meals of solids and nursing and/or bottles. They should be able to easily consume enough food to continue growing at a good rate. They should also be on a consistent scheduled feeding routine, if not please refer to our Nutrition Chapter (page 221). Dropping any nighttime feedings should occur at a faster pace. Parents try to encourage feedings during the day in the hopes that the baby will sleep longer at night. You will increase those odds by eliminating the night feedings. It is only by decreasing the night feedings that your baby will begin to consume more during the day.

This is the point, where although bottle/nursing will still be a significant part of their daily intake of nutrients, solids will slowly start becoming their primary source of calories the closer you get to twelve months. Even with what seems like less ounces/minutes they feed overall; your baby will be satisfied enough to sleep through the night. Parents often get hung up on their baby's last bottle, don't. If they've eaten enough during their other three feedings, they should be just fine. In time, all your baby will need is a few sips of milk in a sippy cup, before bed. Eventually, just a few sips of water will suffice.

As far as teething, if your baby has an average day, feeding well and showing no signs of pain/discomfort, it is okay to begin training. Our experience has shown that the most painful and disruptive teeth are the front two upper and lower teeth, they often get in the way of sleep training. After the gums have been broken by a tooth, the ones that follow are much less eventful. Although every baby is different, on average, it becomes easier and less disruptive to your baby's routine.

Baby is safe

Your baby should be on a flat mattress, with secure fitted sheets. We suggest using the Angel monitor if you are not room sharing. It will make the transition to sleeping in a separate room easier on parents. Breathable net bumpers may be used, especially if your baby tends to get their arms or legs caught in the crib slats. We recommend removing any mobiles or in crib toys. Finally, make sure their crib is in its lowest setting to prevent your baby from falling when standing up and to discourage trying to climb out.

It should be safe for your baby to have a lovie or a little soft small blankie that can be used as an emotional support object. Avoid loose buttons or other decorative features that can come loose with time (potential choking hazard). We also recommend avoiding weighted blankies even if they promise to encourage better sleep.

Baby is in an environment conducive to sleep

Before you begin training, we recommend you spend 10-15 minutes in your baby's nursery after your baby falls asleep. This will allow you to see what your baby sees if they do wake up, during the night. Any sources of direct light should be covered. You will notice that ambient light will seep through blinds, under the door. That's why these 10-15 minutes of assessment are so important, it will allow your eyes to adjust.

New guidelines suggest that your baby's nursery should be between 65- and 72-degrees Fahrenheit. A cooler environment is more conducive to sleep. During seasonal changes, parents should be especially conscious of overnight temperatures since they can affect internal room temperature and humidity.

As for sounds, at this point, your baby will benefit most from instrumental lullabies or lullabies without lyrics. You may still use natural sounds if you prefer. In our experience, instrumental lullabies seem to be slightly more effective at helping babies to self soothe. We do not recommend white noise since it only serves to mask outside sounds but does not provide the emotional comfort natural sounds do.

Baby is in an emotional place where they can learn

When training begins, trust your knowledge of your baby. We always suggest that parents consider starting on a Friday so that the most difficult nights occur when they don't have work or other considerations. This also frees parents to work together so that they may take turns during the overnight hours. Remember, sleep is a primary need, you need sleep too!

Establishing a nighttime routine is essential to the overall process. It will physically signal to your baby it's time to slow down and ease them into a more restful mood. Your nighttime routine can include bathing (not necessarily done every night), changing them into pajamas, reading 2-3 short books (soft light should be used if possible), singing songs, anything that you really enjoy doing that is not overly stimulating. Remember though, that consistency is key. Choose activities that you wouldn't mind doing frequently. The final step in your nighttime routine should be the final feeding so plan accordingly.

Once you've gone through the nighttime routine, they should be put in the crib awake. Lights should then be turned off and parents should exit the nursery. It's very important that you put your baby in their crib awake if and when possible. The beginning of the night is the best time to introduce changes. If your baby is asleep before you place them in their crib, they will miss the opportunity to develop the skills necessary for them to fall asleep independently in the middle of the night. Be aware, the first time you try putting your baby down awake, and they have not had the opportunity to fall asleep without assistance, it will take, on average, 45 to 90 minutes for them to fall asleep independently.

Once you place them in their crib, begin using the five-minute rule. Wait to start the timer until their cry reaches an intense level (the monitor line should be between orange and red). If after five minutes they've maintained this intense level of crying and have shown no signs of trying to self soothe, you can go in for three minutes. The purpose of you going in is twofold, first to fix whatever your baby can not fix themselves (dirty diaper, light turned on, stuck in odd position), second to help calm your baby from a place where they're too emotional back down to a level where you can see that they've gotten ahold of themselves.

When you go in, its ok to shush, pat, softly talk (short reassuring sentences), and (depending on how emotional your baby is) you may pick them up. If you choose to do so, hold them tight and softly reassure them. Try not to rock or sway. Once your baby has calmed for a minute place them back, in a seated position, in their crib and walk out. By now the habits you have reinforced for the last 9 to 12 months are ingrained, and your baby will likely be more emotional than usual. Don't try to force them into sitting or lying down. Let the process happen as it should, in your baby's own timing.

If after three minutes your baby is still crying, place them back in their crib and walk away. Three minutes is the maximum amount of time you want to spend in their room. If at any point your baby stops, before the allotted three minutes, while you are in the nursery, place them back in the crib early. The goal is just to reset them, so they learn to manage themselves. Don't overstay their need.

Repeat throughout the night. The first 20 minutes of your baby's night will almost certainly be intense. It may feel like you going in just makes things worse. That's normal. It is important, that you do so, because that is what will break the pattern of behavior that has been created before now. Your baby is under the assumption that the louder they cry the faster you'll respond. Don't be surprised if your baby wails louder and moves around in protest when you first enter their nursery and when you place them back in their crib. At the three-minute mark, you must place your baby back in their crib even if they are still crying. It's important to keep in mind that the 3-minute reset is as much for you as it is for your baby. This is a highly emotional process and the time spent reassuring your baby is also time for you to gather yourself.

Usually after 20 minutes of using the five-minute rule, you will notice that your baby will start making better use of the five minutes. This is where you will really begin to see signs of self-soothing. If, at any point,

Room to Grow

your baby shows signs of calming, crying slows for longer than 60 seconds or they begin to try to physically self soothe, i.e. going from a standing to a seating position, trying to suck on their hands, or trying to find the pacifier, reset the timer. If you're at all unsure if you should go in, add another minute to the timer. You don't want to go in just before your baby has the aha moment.

While you're out of the room, monitoring, take the time to calm yourself. We cannot overstate how emotional this can be on a parent, make sure to take your feelings into account. Your baby can feel your stress. Take the five minutes to center yourself and to calm as much as possible so that your baby can sense your confidence when you do enter the room.

The first night, at this age group, the average baby will take 45 minutes to two hours to fully calm and fall asleep. The first 20-30 minutes will be the most intense. You will notice that after the first 20-30 minutes the intensity of the crying will diminish and the length of time it takes to reach the full five minutes will increase, i.e. you'll be able to reset your timer and will need to enter less frequently. Once your baby falls asleep, the consecutive wake ups will be less intense and will not last as long. The average time of a middle of the night wake up is usually between 15 to 20 minutes. This should be the case until the 11th hour.

The first night will be your baseline and will help measure your baby's progress. Write down everything during this process, when they wake up, how long they cry, how intense, etc. This will help you see progress when things are toughest. The five-minute rule should be used until the 11th hour. At that point you will want

Chapter Four

to begin using the 15-minute rule. Ideally you will do at least two rounds of the 15-minute rule before beginning your baby's day. Their scheduled feeding time shouldn't change if you decide to pick them up early.

You should see significant improvement nightly as your baby practices. If the first night of training is fairly easy, prepare yourself for the second night, this is supposed to be challenging. By this age your baby should understand that change is happening. If the first night is easy the second night will often be more difficult because of this understanding. The third night is where you should start to see definitive improvement.

In the first three days of training, after the 11th hour, depending on how upset your baby is, its ok to stop the training at this hour. Again, this only applies for the first few days of training. We don't want to overwhelm your baby or you so this is a temporary allowance that we make in order to keep you motivated. There are three things we are trying to teach your baby: how to go to sleep, how to stay asleep, and how to wake up happy. How to wake up happy is the last step of the training. It is where we address the 11th hour. Early wake ups are the most challenging part of the sleep training process. This is why it is so beneficial to long term sleep skills. This 11th hour will also help with the nap training, since this hour most closely resembles their naps.

After the three days of training, you should see enough progress during the night, to start applying the 15-minute rule, to that 11th hour. Your baby by now should be having long stretches of restorative sleep, she will wake up somewhat rested and happy. Don't rush in, the main purpose of the 15-minute rule is to give your baby a chance to learn patience. From the moment your baby stops "talking" and starts whimpering (does not have to be full on crying) where you see that they're beginning to escalate, start your timer. After 15 minutes, go in. You have three minutes to assess the situation and help them calm slightly. After the three minutes, leave the room. Do another round of 15 minutes. If they're still crying, you can go in and start their day. Ideally, they would maintain their scheduled feeding, so even though you're picking them up a little early try to hold off the feeding. We suggest at least one round of the 15-minute rule. Two rounds of 15-minute "patience practice" are ideal. Let the intensity of the crying and your baby's mood determine how many rounds of 15-minute practice you'll do.

When you do decide to start their day, turn on the lights, open the blinds, and start talking to your baby in a happy voice, i.e. "Good morning! What's all this fuss about? You did such a great job!". Ideally, we want your baby to calm slightly before you pick them up. Show them with nonverbal communication that everything is ok. At this age, their first reaction will be an increase in their crying because they think you're going to leave again. By waiting until your baby calms slightly, you will teach them they do not need to cry in order to get picked up. They will start to understand that the morning routine means the day is starting and in time, they will smile when you come in. We want to start rewarding positive behaviors.

Chapter Four

Things to expect during this developmental phase

Sitting up in crib

At this age your baby should be able to fully sit upright. Going from a seated position to a prone position is a skill. Parents have a tendency to place their baby laying down in their crib. Take this opportunity to help them practice. At their initial bedtime, place them in their crib so that they're sitting.

You may find there comes a time where your baby is sitting down crying and falls asleep sitting up (having refused to lay down). It's up to your baby to figure out how to go from sitting down to laying down. When you first begin training you can try to coax them into laying down. Ultimately your baby will have to decide to lay themselves down. That will be the real breakthrough.

Standing in crib

You can reach this developmental stage if you're just starting sleep training or if your baby has already been sleeping trained and has otherwise slept well during the night. If your baby is already sleeping through the night and suddenly wakes up and immediately stand ups, chances are they will start to cry. When babies first start to stand up, they tend to lock their knees, they have not yet learned to bend their knees to plop down.

Here, we encourage you (during the first three nights) to place your baby from a standing to sitting position. Let that be a warning to work the following days in practicing plopping down. Practice during the day will make the process more efficient. Once you see that your baby begins to gain the ability to plop down during the day, it's time to start raising your expectations in the middle of the nights. Developmental stages, like this one, should not disrupt sleep for longer than three nights.

If you're just starting to sleep train, this phase may be very challenging. As your baby stands up and refuses to sit, use the five-minute rule. When you go in, if you pick your baby up, place them back in their crib sitting down. By now they should have mastered laying down from a sitting position. Chances are they will stand right back up anyway. It's to be expected, keep using the 5-minute rule.

If your baby falls asleep standing up, go in and sit them down. The goal is to guide your baby to decide to sit and then lay down on their own. Safety always comes first. Resist the urge to lay your baby down. While it is tempting to gain short term relief it will greatly slow the learning process. The more your baby practices on their own the faster they will learn.

Throwing objects from crib

You may find that once standing your baby begins to throw things out of their crib, often their pacifier or lovie. This will cause their crying to increase. We recommend that the first three times that this happens you place the item back into their crib. If they continue to throw the item out of the crib, then we recommend that you leave them where they are. We do not want your baby to learn that throwing the toy will get your attention. If they throw the toy, we want them to learn that eventually, they will have to go without it.

Responds to verbal requests

At this age, your baby will begin to understand what you're saying to them. Its best to keep instructions short and concise. A gentle yet firm tone should be used. Parents should begin to develop the habit of verbally communicating with their baby. As they get older, this will become the primary way you can comfort your baby in the middle of the night.

Social with family, shy with strangers

In order to minimize the shyness your baby can develop during this stage you should try to encourage the people in your baby's life to participate in this process. Parents should take turns putting baby to bed and responding in the middle of the nights. Grandparents, aunts, uncles, and other caregivers should also be incorporated when possible after training.

If your baby shows a preference or is more dependent towards one parent, we recommend that the other parent handle the first few nights of training. This will make the overall process easier on your baby. Once your baby has shown some improvement you can reintroduce the other parent to establish the new pattern of behavior. Your baby should be able to perform well with anyone.

Chapter Four

7:00 AM – 7:00 PM Schedule
Nine to Twelve Months

7:00 – 7:15 AM – Wake up

7:00 – 7:30 AM – First feeding

7:30 – 9:00 AM – Activity time

9:00 – 10:30 AM – Morning nap

10:30 – 11:00 AM – Activity time

11:00 – 11:30 AM – Second feeding

11:30 – 1:00 PM – Activity time

1:00 – 3:00 PM – Afternoon nap

3:00 – 3:30 PM – Third feeding

3:30 – 6:30 PM – Activity time

6:30 – 7:00 PM – Fourth feeding

7:00 PM – Bedtime

Room to Grow

Babycoach Case Study

Laurel was 10 months and had just learned to stand up. Her parents had used the Babycoach method and had a great sleeper in Laurel since she was 10 weeks old. One of their biggest problems was that now she was waking up several times at night standing in her crib, knees locked and screaming.

After a week of the new behavior, she also started exhibiting crying spells every time her mom left the room throughout the night. After a few weeks of the new pattern of behavior, Laurel started to throw her pacifier out of the crib at nap time and started to increasingly cry during both naps. The exhaustion and anxiety started taking a toll on the whole family.

How we trained Laurel

We started by having her parents spend three days with a lot of standing/plopping down practice. On the night of the third day, once we noticed that she had become very efficient at plopping down, we started expecting more effort from Laurel and began re-training her to sleep through the night.

We began by having her parents place her in her crib standing up after they had gone through their nighttime routine. Our goal was to have Laurel use the skills she had developed over the last three days to consciously decide to sit and then lay herself down. Her parents then exited the room and we began using the three- minute rule. We decided to use the three-minute rule instead of the recommended five-minute rule since her crying was especially intense and her mother was very sensitive to it. On the first night, Laurel eventually fell asleep standing up and we needed to go in and lie her down. On the second and third nights she ultimately laid herself down and fell sleep.

To address her throwing her pacifier out of her crib we began by having her parents place five pacifiers in her crib before bedtime. While we were using the three-minute rule, if we noticed that she had thrown a pacifier from her crib we made sure to remove it from her room entirely. The first two nights, Laurel threw every one of the five pacifiers out of her crib. After the second night she realized that throwing them now meant that she would have to go without. On night three she threw only four of her pacifiers and on night four she only threw one. By the end of the training period she learned to stop throwing them entirely.

As for her naps, the nighttime sleep training did improve her naps significantly but didn't solve the problem entirely. We had her parents begin using the five-minute rule during the first half of her nap and the 15-minute patience practice rule during the second. We also replicated the rules we had put in place during her nights, placing her in her crib standing up and not replacing pacifiers if thrown. It took another four days after she was fully sleeping through the night again for us to see even more improvement in her naps.

We suggested the parents to maintain a practice routine for the two-week reinforcement period to really lock in the results.

Chapter Five

Twelve to Eighteen Months

If your baby has slept through the night for a period during their first year, but you feel sleep is not where it should be, go back and use the four basic steps. Your baby should revert to what they know when the rules are reinforced consistently

If this is the first time that you're training your baby, be aware that your baby has not developed basic sleep skills. Instead, they've developed habits that are going to make sleep training especially challenging. We encourage you to look at sleep training as a great opportunity to finally instill the optimal foundation for good sleeping habits.

If you have never sleep trained your baby. The habits you want to change have been developed and reinforced for an extended period. Your baby is old enough to understand that changes are taking place and they will resist those changes. Extended periods of crying, anger, heated pleas, frustration, should all be expected for at least the first week of training. Expect your baby to use words to evoke an emotional response. "Mama", "Daddy", "I'm sorry", etc. Whatever bad habits they have developed, expect them to get slightly worse or more pronounced, before getting better.

Some toddlers will exhibit changes in their daily behavior while sleep training. You may notice that they are quieter or more clingy than usual. This is very normal while they work to understand why the changes are occurring and how those changes will affect them.

Before beginning the training process, take an honest assessment of their starting point. Be honest about the extent of the issues you're facing. Its only by being very honest of your starting point, that you will appreciate how much effort your toddler will invest and how much progress they will make. Chances are you might have formed the same habits as your baby. Part of this step, is to also take stock. It can be very difficult to admit the role you've played in developing these habits. Don't be too hard on yourself but be honest. Again, it's only when you really see your beginning that you can appreciate the end result. You are going to learn and grow just as much if not more than your toddler.

Some parents may become frustrated if the training does not occur as quickly as they want it to. This is a learning process. Every child learns at their own pace. These habits did not form overnight, they will not be broken overnight. Be patient enough to see results. You cannot rush the process.

Chapter Five

How to sleep train at this age

Baby is healthy

As always make sure your baby is healthy before beginning to sleep train. Teething should be much less of an issue. Always make sure to keep your pediatrician up to date.

By this point, your baby no longer needs to feed in the middle of the night. You can fully eliminate all nighttime feeds in one step. Remember, whatever calories they eat at night, they will not be motivated to eat during the day.

Baby is safe

At this age, your baby should be walking or nearly able to walk. Be aware that the ability to stand and walk could lead to your baby trying to climb out of their crib during the training process. Take every appropriate measure to ensure your baby's safety if you notice signs of your baby attempting to do so. Anything that could help them climb should be removed from their crib, bumpers, pillows, etc. A lovie or small stuffed animal should be the only thing in the crib.

Make sure that the crib is placed away from blinds, loose electrical cords, corded blinds, etc. Your baby will have plenty of time to observe their environment. Anything within grabbing distance should be moved. They *will* try to grab it.

Their crib should be at the lowest setting by now to discourage climbing. The sleep sack should no longer be needed and may get in their way. We recommend footie pajamas, or something similar, that allows for full range of motion.

Baby is in an environment conducive to sleep

Baby's this age benefit from having a nightlight. The light should be placed behind a piece of furniture so that the light is diffused. You want to be conscious of how bright the nightlight is, opt for fainter light if possible.

We suggest playing lullabies with lyrics throughout the night since your baby is in the beginnings of their speech development phase. This will be the most effective soothing noise you can use by far. You can also choose lullabies in different languages or numbers or letters recited slowly. We want to use their curiosity towards speech to help distract them if they begin to cry overnight. The volume should be at a lower setting, this way they're motivated to quiet in order to hear what is being said.

Chapter Five

Baby is in an emotional place where they can learn

When training begins, trust your knowledge of your baby. We always suggest that parents consider starting on a Friday so that the most difficult nights occur when they don't have work or other considerations. This also frees parents to work together so that they may take turns during the overnight hours. Remember, sleep is a primary need, you need sleep too!

Establishing a nighttime routine is essential to the overall process. It will physically signal to your baby that it's time to slow down and ease them into a more restful mood. Your nighttime routine can include bathing (not necessarily done every night), changing them into pajamas, reading 2-3 short books (soft light should be used if possible), singing songs, anything that you really enjoy doing that is not overly stimulating. Remember though, that consistency is key. Choose activities that you wouldn't mind doing frequently. The final step in your nighttime routine should be the final feeding so plan accordingly.

Once you've gone through the nighttime routine, they should be put in the crib awake. Lights should then be turned off and parents should exit the nursery. It's very important that you put your baby in their crib awake if and when possible. The beginning of the night is the best time to introduce changes. If your baby is asleep before you place them in their crib, they will miss the opportunity to develop the skills necessary for them to fall back asleep independently in the middle of the night. Be aware, the first time you try putting your baby down awake, and they have not had the opportunity to fall asleep without assistance, it will take them, on average, 45 to 90 minutes for them to fall asleep independently.

Once you place them in their crib, begin using the five-minute rule. Wait to start the timer until their cry reaches an intense level (the monitor line should be between orange and red). If after five minutes they've maintained this intense level of crying and have shown no signs of trying to self soothe, you can go in for three minutes. The purpose of you going in is twofold, first to fix whatever your baby can not fix themselves (dirty diaper, light turned on, stuck in odd position), second to help calm your baby from a place where they're too emotional back down to a level where you can see that they've gotten ahold of themselves.

Verbal communication will be your most effective tool at this age. You want to be compassionate and reassuring, "It's okay baby, it's okay" while reminding them what you're expecting from them "it's time to go night-night", "It's time to sleep", etc. Your tone will determine how effective your verbal communication is. You want to use a kind but firm tone; you're telling your baby what you want them to do. You're not trying to negotiate with or cajole them. Those days are gone, you must be their rock. Your tone will let them know that you mean what you say. If you need to physically reassure them try not to rock or sway when you pick them up. Keep stimulation to a minimum. Once your baby has calmed for a minute place them back, in a seated position, in their crib and walk out. By now the habits you have reinforced for the last twelve to eighteen months are ingrained, and your baby will likely be more emotional than usual. Don't try to force

Chapter Five

them into sitting or lying down. Let the process happen as it should, in your baby's own timing.

If after three minutes your toddler is still crying, place them back in their crib and walk away. Three minutes is the maximum amount of time you want to spend in their room. If at any point your baby stops, before the allotted three minutes, while you are in the nursery, place them back in the crib early. The goal is just to reset them, so they learn to manage themselves. Don't overstay their need.

Repeat throughout the night. The first 30 minutes of your baby's night will almost certainly be intense. It may feel like you going in just makes things worse. That's normal. It is important, that you do so, because that is what will break the pattern of behavior that has been created before now. Your baby is under the assumption that the louder they cry the faster you'll respond. Don't be surprised if your baby wails louder and moves around in protest when you first enter their nursery and when you place them back in their crib. At the three-minute mark, you must place your baby back in their crib even if they are still crying. It's important to keep in mind that the 3-minute reset is as much for you as it is for your baby. This is a highly emotional process and the time spent reassuring your baby is also time for you to reassure yourself.

If you notice that your action, going in, is causing an immediate reaction by your baby, i.e. your baby stops crying as soon as you open their door, that's a sign that your baby understands their crying gets a specific result. You should change your reaction. Consider speaking to them through the monitor or sending in the other parent. You want to respond in a way they're not expecting. If your baby can immediately stop crying as soon as they get a desired response, that should tell you that their cry is not an emotional or need cry but a willful one. They're demanding that response. Use this knowledge to shore up your resolve and stay committed to being consistent.

Usually after 30 minutes of using the five-minute rule, you will notice that your baby will start making better use of the five minutes. This is where you will really begin to see signs of self-soothing. If, at any point, your baby shows signs of calming, crying slows for longer than 60 seconds or they begin to try to physically self soothe, i.e. going from a standing to a seating position, trying to suck on their hands, or trying to find the pacifier, reset the timer. If you're at all unsure if you should go in, add another minute to the timer. You don't want to go in just before your baby has the aha moment.

While you're out of the room, monitoring, take the time to calm yourself. We cannot overstate how emotional this can be on a parent, make sure to take your feelings into account. Your baby can feel your stress. Take the five minutes to center yourself and to calm as much as possible so that your baby can sense your confidence when you do enter the room.

The first night, at this age group, the average baby will take between one to two hours to fully calm and fall asleep. The first 20-30 minutes will be the most intense. You will notice that after the first 20-30 minutes the intensity of the crying will diminish and the length of time it takes to reach the full five minutes will increase, i.e. you'll be able to reset your timer and will need to enter less frequently. Once your baby falls asleep, the consecutive wake ups will be less intense and will not last as long. The average time of a middle of the night wake up is usually between 15 to 20 minutes. This should be the case until the 11th hour.

The first night will be your baseline and will help measure your baby's progress. Write down everything during this process, when they wake up, how long they cry, how intense, etc. This will help you see progress when things are toughest. The five-minute rule should be used until the 11th hour. At that point you will want to begin using the 15-minute rule. Ideally you will do at least two rounds of the 15-minute rule before beginning your baby's day. Their scheduled feeding time shouldn't change if you decide to pick them up early.

You should see significant improvement nightly as your baby practices. If the first night of training is fairly easy, prepare yourself for the second night, this is supposed to be challenging. By this age your baby should understand that change is happening. If the first night is easy the second night will often be more difficult because of this understanding. The third night is where you should start to see definitive improvement.

In the first three days of training, after the 11th hour, depending on how upset your toddler was, its ok to stop the training at this hour. Again, this only applies for the first few days of training. We don't want to overwhelm your baby or you, so this is a temporary allowance we make in order to keep you motivated. There are three things we are trying to teach your baby: how to go to sleep, how to stay asleep, and how to wake up happy. How to wake up happy is the last step of the training. It is where we address the 11th hour. Early wake ups are the most challenging part of the sleep training process. This is why it is so beneficial to long term sleep skills. This 11th hour will also help with the nap training, since this hour most closely resembles their naps.

After the three days of training, you should see enough progress during the night, to start applying the 15-minute rule, to that 11th hour. Your baby by now should be having long stretches of restorative sleep, she will wake up somewhat rested and happy. Don't rush in, the main purpose of the 15-minute rule is to give your baby a chance to learn patience. From the moment your baby stops "talking" and starts whimpering (does not have to be full on crying) where you see that they're beginning to escalate, start your timer. After 15 minutes, go in. You have three minutes to assess the situation and help them calm slightly. After the three minutes, leave the room. Do another round of 15 minutes. If they're still crying, you can go in and start their day. Ideally, they would maintain their scheduled feeding, so even though you're picking them up a little early try to hold off the feeding. We suggest at least one round of the 15-minute rule. Two rounds of 15-minute "patience practice" are ideal. Let the intensity of the crying and your baby's mood determine how many rounds of 15-minute practice you'll do.

When you do decide to start their day, turn on the lights, open the blinds, and start talking to your baby in a happy voice, i.e. "Good morning! What's all this fuss about? You did such a great job!". Ideally, we want your baby to calm slightly before you pick them up. Show them with nonverbal communication that everything is ok. At this age, their first reaction will be an increase in their crying because they think you're going to leave again. By waiting until your baby calms slightly, you will teach them they do not need to cry in order to get picked up. They will start to understand that the morning routine means the day is starting and in time, they will smile when you come in. We want to start rewarding positive behaviors.

Things you can expect during this phase

Walking

You can reach this developmental stage if you're just starting sleep training or if your baby has already been sleeping trained and has otherwise slept well during the night. If your baby is already sleeping through the night and suddenly wakes up and immediately stand ups, chances are they will start to cry. When babies first start to stand up, they tend to lock their knees, they have not yet learned to bend their knees to plop down.

We encourage you (during the first three nights) to place your baby from a standing to sitting position. Work the following days, encouraging them to practice plopping down. Practice will to make the process more efficient. Once you see that your baby begins to gain the ability to plop down during the day, it's time to start raising your expectations in the middle of the nights. Developmental stages, like this one, should not disrupt sleep for longer than three nights. Since most babies learn to walk months after they've learned to stand, they should learn how to sit themselves back down very quickly.

If you're just starting to sleep train, this phase may be very challenging. As your baby stands up and refuses to sit, use the five-minute rule. When you go in, if pick your baby up, place them back in their crib sitting down. By now they should have mastered laying down from a sitting position. Chances are that they will stand right back up anyway. It's to be expected, keep using the 5-minute rule.

If your baby falls asleep standing up, go in and sit them down. The goal is to guide your baby to decide to sit and then lay down on their own. Safety always comes first. Resist the urge to lay your baby down. While it is tempting to gain short term relief it will greatly slow the learning process. The more your baby practices on their own the faster they will learn.

Enhanced ability to reach and grab

Parents should move everything within grabbing distance. We want to remove temptation where we can. Expect toddlers to be extra active during the end of the day and during the nighttime routine. Nighttime routine might need to be moved slightly earlier or given more time all together to give the baby time to wind down.

You may find that your baby uses their increased mobility to resist bedtime. Toddlers will try to walk or run away from their bedroom. Outwit your little one, so that they have limited options. If they're prone to running out of the room, start closing the door during their routine. If they're prone to trying to open their door, babyproof the handle.

Shows strong dependency on primary caregiver, increased difficult separating

Because babies can show a strong preference for their primary caregiver, especially at this age. We suggest that the other parent take the lead for the first few nights of sleep training. This will help make the transition easier emotionally for both parent and baby.

This strategy should also be used if your baby calls for a specific parent. If baby wants Mom, then Dad should go in. Sleep training is all about challenging your baby. We want to respond to their needs but not always their wants. If they physically need you, then either parent should work. If they're only wanting your help, they'll insist on the specific parent and only them, hence training.

Shows difficulty quieting and relaxing into sleep

Babies at this age are easily stimulated, so you may find that your baby will have trouble settling and falling asleep. It's important that parents plan for this with quieter activities at the end of the day. This will give your baby a prolonged period where they can ease into a more restful state. At the same time, use the rest of their day to plan more physically stimulating activities so that they're tired enough at the end of the day to fall asleep.

Always wants to have caregiver to be around

You may notice that your baby is more emotional during the day following the first few nights of training. Within a week or so you should notice that your baby is back to their normal happy self. Provide plenty of emotional support and reassurance during the day. While this is very normal, it is difficult emotionally on parents. Spoil them, and yourselves, with extra cuddles during the day.

Points and vocalizes to indicate wants

Babies can throw their soothing toys or pacifiers when highly emotional. At this age, they will indicate that they want these items back. Pick up the thrown item three times. After the third time, leave the item on the floor or take them out of the room entirely. We want your baby to learn how to self soothe, not that throwing their lovie will get the response they want. Once your baby sees that they will not always get their toy back they will quickly learn to stop throwing things when upset. This is an ideal time to start introducing your baby to actions having consequences.

Does not respond to verbal persuasion, short simple directions are best

Keep directions short and concise. Your tone is just as, if not more, important than what you say. Be firm. Be direct. You're not trying to coerce your baby to sleep, you're telling them what you're expecting.

Express autonomy through defiance

If you are beginning sleep training during this age, your baby will resist change. They are smart and will understand that things are changing, and not in a way that favors their wants. They will dig in their little heels, be prepared emotionally. Once you begin training, be consistent. Follow through long enough to see results. These habits weren't created in one night, they will not be changed in one.

Vocalizes more than cries for attention

As your baby's vocabulary expands, they are going to use phrases such as "mommy", "daddy", "help", "please", "I'm sorry". It will be very challenging for you emotionally. We cannot overstate that. Always remind yourself that you have your child's best interest in mind and that you are trying to do what is best for them.

7:00 AM – 7:00 PM Schedule

Twelve to Eighteen Months

7:00 – 7:15 AM – Wake up

7:00 – 7:30 AM – First feeding

7:30 – 9:00 AM – Activity time

9:00 – 10:00/10:30 AM – Morning nap

10:30 – 11:00 AM – Activity time

11:00 – 11:30 AM – Second feeding

11:30 – 1:00 PM – Activity time

1:00 – 3:00 PM – Afternoon nap

3:00 – 3:30 PM – Third feeding

3:30 – 6:30 PM – Activity time

6:30 – 7:00 PM – Fourth feeding

7:00 PM – Bedtime

Chapter Five

Babycoach Case Study

15-month old twin boys, Clark and Jonathan, had never fully developed the ability to sleep independently. During their first eight months, they usually slept seven to eight hours while swaddled. Once they outgrew the swaddle, their parents relied on sleep suits that restricted movement and eventually double swaddled. They eventually outgrew all options and started sleeping four to five hours.

When they reached about 14 months, their sleep started to suffer again as they started to learn to walk. At that time their parents tried to let them cry it out. Clark and Jonathan were so motivated when crying that they learned to climb out of their cribs. Because they were so physical, the book case, night stand, and their dresser also became a danger.

How we trained Clark and Jonathan

When Karina and Allen contacted us, we immediately suggested a crib tent, as our experience has shown babies tend to welcome the feeling of coziness that comes with the tent for sleep. We installed the tents during the nighttime routine of the first night of training. Both boys immediately took to the tent and didn't try to climb out of the crib on the first night. Jonathan tried on the second and Clark on the third. However, after an attempt or two, it dissuaded them from trying again.

We then suggested introducing lullabies with lyrics to occupy their mind and help them relax enough to fall asleep. Karina ultimately chose lullabies in French, since they wanted them to learn French as well as English. We set the lullabies a bit louder than ideal on the first night to catch their attention, and then lowered the volume on the second and third nights until we reached the lower ideal volume. We also noticed on the first night that the device lit up when the playlist ended and started repeating, so we made sure to cover the screen entirely after the first instance.

We also encouraged them to try to keep both naps even though the twins were starting to show signs of wanting to drop the first nap. We suggested shortening the morning nap from 90 minutes to one hour. Although the signs were there, they were not quite ready to manage longer periods of awake time without their other periods of sleep suffering.

After the initial training period, we had their parents be very consistent through the two-week reinforcement period.

Chapter Six

Eighteen to Twenty-Four Months

If you have sleep trained your baby with our method, as always refer back to the four basics. However, understand that retraining at this age will be more difficult. Your baby is old enough and smart enough to understand that they had two very different scenarios (trained sleep and unrestricted sleep). They understand that they highly prefer the unrestricted scenario. They will resist the training. Be prepared to withstand a lot of frustration and anger.

If you have never sleep trained your baby. The habits you want to change have been developed and reinforced for an extended period. Your baby is old enough to understand that changes are taking place and they will resist those changes. Extended periods of crying, anger, heated pleas, frustration, should all be expected for at least the first week of training. Some toddlers will exhibit changes in their daily behavior while sleep training. You may notice that they are quieter or more clingy than usual. This is very normal while they work to understand why the changes are occurring and how those changes will affect them.

Before beginning the training process, take an honest assessment of their starting point. Be honest about the extent of the issues you're facing. Its only by being very honest of your starting point, that you will appreciate how much effort your toddler will invest and how much progress they will make. Chances are you might have formed the same habits as your baby. Part of this step, is to also take stock. It can be very difficult to admit the role you've played in developing these habits. Don't be too hard on yourself but be honest. Again, it's only when you really see your beginning that you can appreciate the end result. You are going to learn and grow just as much if not more than your toddler.

Some parents may become frustrated if the training does not occur as quickly as they want it to. This is a learning process. Every child learns at their own pace. These habits did not form overnight, they will not be broken overnight. Be patient enough to see results. You cannot rush the process.

Chapter Six

How to sleep train at this age

Baby is healthy

By this point, your toddler should no longer need to feed in the middle of the night. Any feedings are habit based and can be dropped immediately. Weaning is not necessary. Any feedings should be eliminated within a night or two at most.

Teething should no longer be an issue. If your baby still has teeth coming in, they should be used to the sensation. It should not interfere with sleep training.

Finally look for any signs of illness before training begins. This is an age where we often see children start going to daycare if they haven't already. That often comes with a maelstrom of germs and illnesses. If they were sick recently but seem otherwise better, it's fine to sleep train if there are minor lingering symptoms, i.e. stuffy or runny nose. If your baby is showing real signs of illness, i.e. fever, lack of appetite, etc., contact your pediatrician and hold of sleep training until they're feeling better.

Baby is safe

Be aware that the ability to stand and walk could lead to your baby trying to climb out of their crib during the training process. Parents should take every appropriate measure to ensure their baby's safety, if you notice signs of your baby attempting to do so.

There is a greater chance of your baby trying to climb out of their crib at this age. Anything that could help them climb should be removed from their crib, this can include bumpers, pillows, or larger stuffed animals. Take time before training to observe their environment. Think of the possibilities while keeping in mind that your baby will be highly motivated. Whatever can become a safety risk should be eliminated.

A lovie or a couple of small stuffed animal should be the only thing in their crib. It's very easy to go overboard in this area, especially if your little one has many to choose from. Try to limit stuffed animals or friends to no more than one or two at most.

If you find that your toddler persists in trying to climb out of their crib and their safety is a concern, consider a crib tent or be ready to transfer them into a toddler bed early. Ensure that their crib is lowered to its lowest setting as this will also make climbing more difficult. Make sure that the crib is placed away from blinds, loose electrical cords, corded blinds. Your baby will have plenty of time to observe their environment. Anything within grabbing distance should be moved. They *will* try to grab it.

A sleep sack should no longer be needed and may get in their way. Footie pajamas, or something similar that allows for full range of motion, are ideal. If you're eliminating the sleep sack and are worried about your toddler's comfort, try layering clothes or heavier fabrics that better retain heat. Recently, hybrid sleep sacks

Chapter Six

have become available. These sacks feature openings for your toddler's feet so that they can move more freely. They are an option if you feel your toddler is not quite ready to eliminate the sleep sack fully.

Baby is in an environment conducive to sleep

Toddler's this age benefit from having a nightlight. The light should be placed behind a piece of furniture so that the light is diffused. You want to be conscious of how bright the nightlight is, choose a faint light if possible. It should also be placed as far from their bed as possible, since we don't want it to disrupt their sleep unnecessarily.

At this point we suggest that you use lullabies with lyrics since your baby is in middle of their speech development phase. You can also use audiobooks or a recording of you reading books. If your baby is being exposed to a second or third language, this is a great time to incorporate new languages. If parents decide to use a recording of their own voice, books, letters, numbers can all be used just keep in mind that a low and steady rhythm is more conducive to sleep. We want to use their curiosity towards speech to help distract them if they begin to cry overnight. The volume should be slightly lower than previous noises, this way they are motivated to quiet in order to hear what is being said.

Baby is in an emotional place where they can learn

When training begins trust your knowledge of your toddler. We always suggest that parents consider starting on a Friday so that the most difficult nights occur when they don't have work or other considerations. This also frees parents to work together so that they may take turns during the overnight hours. Remember, sleep is a primary need, you need sleep too!

Establishing a nighttime routine is essential to the overall process. It will physically signal to your toddler that it's time to slow down and ease them into a more restful mood. Your nighttime routine can include bathing (not necessarily done every night), changing them into pajamas, reading 2-3 short books (soft light should be used if possible), singing songs, anything that you really enjoy doing that is not overly stimulating. Remember though, that consistency is key. Choose activities that you wouldn't mind doing frequently. One of the final steps should be brushing their teeth. Afterwards, only offer sips of water. The final step of the nighttime routine should be one more book or song and tucking them in.

Once you've gone through the nighttime routine, put them down in their crib awake. Lights should then be turned off and exit the nursery. It's very important that you put your baby in their crib awake whenever possible. The beginning of the night is the best time to introduce changes. If your baby is asleep before you place them in their crib, they will miss the opportunity to develop the skills necessary for them to fall back asleep independently in the middle of the night.

Chapter Six

The first time you try putting your toddler down awake, and they have not had the opportunity to fall asleep without assistance, it will take them, on average, 45 minutes to 90 minutes to fall asleep independently. The first two to three nights of training will often be the most difficult, but you should be able to notice progress by the fourth night.

Once you place them in their crib, begin using the five-minute rule. Wait to start the timer until their cry reaches an intense level, the monitor line should be between orange and red. If, after five minutes, they've maintained this intense level of crying and have shown no signs of trying to self soothe, you can go in for three minutes. The purpose of you going in is twofold, first to fix whatever your toddler can not fix themselves, i.e. a dirty diaper, a light left on, stuck in odd position, etc., and second to help them calm from a place where they're too emotional back down to a level where you can see that they've gotten ahold of themselves and can try again.

At this age your most effective tool when resetting will be verbal communication. Be compassionate while reassuring them "It's okay, it's okay" while reminding them what you're expecting from them "it's time to go night-night", "It's time to sleep", "Lay down and go to sleep", etc. Your tone will determine how effective your verbal communication is, so use a firm tone. You're telling your toddler what you want them to do, not trying to negotiate with them or cajole them. Those days are gone, you must be their rock. Your tone will let them know that you mean what you say, be firm. This does not mean yelling or shouting, neither of which is a tone that firmly gives direction.

Yelling and shouting are emotional signs that show your toddler that their tactics are working. They're just another way to reinforce negative behaviors.

After verbally resetting them you can say something like "I love you. I'll check on you in in a bit". Close their door and restart your timer. Repeat, repeat, repeat throughout the night. The first 30 minutes of your baby's night will almost certainly be intense. It may feel like you going in is just makes things worse. That's normal. It is important, that you do so, because that is what will break the pattern of behavior that has been created before now. Your little one is under the assumption that the louder they cry the faster you'll respond. Don't be surprised if they wail louder or their behavior worsens when you first enter their nursery and when you start leaving their room. Ultimately, it will be you leaving that really causes them to learn. Limit your time in their room to three minutes at most.

It's important to keep in mind that the three-minute reset is as much for you as it is for your baby. This is a highly emotional process and the time spent reassuring your baby is also time for you to reassure yourself. You are part of this process, your little one is not alone.

Usually after 30 minutes of using the five-minute rule, you will start to notice signs of your toddler trying to self soothe. It's at this point that you should begin to reset your timer if your baby shows signs of calming, crying slows for longer than 60 seconds or they begin to try to physically self soothe, i.e. sit or lay down, find their pacifier, grab their stuffed animal, etc. If you're at all unsure if you should go in, add another minute to the

Chapter Six

timer. You don't want to go in just before your baby has the aha moment.

While you're out of the room, monitoring, take the time to calm yourself. We cannot overstate how emotional this can be on a parent, make sure to take your feelings into account. Your baby can feel your stress. Take the five minutes to center and calm yourself as much as possible so that your baby can sense your confidence when you do enter the room.

Since most parents have tried to sleep train before by this age, you may find yourself tempted to extend the timer beyond five minutes. Don't do it! Whenever you go in to reset your toddler, you are nonverbally telling them that they are not going to get the response they want. You are consistently letting them know that this change is happening and that it will continue to happen. That's what will create the new habit. While it will make the initial change more difficult, it is necessary for long term success. Five minutes is enough time for your toddler to try to self soothe, just enough for you to show that their behavior is not getting the old response, but not enough to let them feel hopeless and give up.

If you notice that your action, going in, is causing an immediate reaction by your little one, i.e. your baby stops crying as soon as you open their door, that's a sign that your toddler has learned that their crying is getting a specific result. You should change your reaction. Consider giving them more than five minutes, speaking to them through the monitor, or sending in the other parent. You want to respond in a way they're not expecting. If your baby can immediately stop crying as soon as they get a desired response, that should tell you that their cry is not an emotional or need cry but a willful one. They're demanding that response. This should be a very clear signal to you to be that much more consistent with the training.

The first night, at this age group, on average a toddler will take 45 minutes to two hours to fully calm and fall asleep. The first 20-30 minutes will be the most intense. You will notice that after the first 20-30 minutes the intensity of the crying will diminish and the length of time it takes to reach the full five minutes will increase, i.e. you'll be able to reset your timer and will need to enter less frequently. Write down everything during this process, when they wake up, how long they cry, how intense, etc. This will help monitor progress. Once your baby falls asleep, the consecutive wake ups will be less intense and will not last as long. The average time of a middle of the night wake up is usually between 15 to 20 minutes. This should be the case until the 11th hour.

The first night will be your baseline and will help you measure your baby's progress. The five-minute rule should be used until the 11th hour. At that point you should use the 15-minute rule. Ideally you will do at least two rounds of the 15-minute rule before beginning your baby's day. Their scheduled feeding time shouldn't change if you decide to pick them up early.

You will see significant improvement nightly as your baby practices. If the first night of training is fairly easy, prepare yourself for the second night, this is supposed to be challenging. At this age your baby understands that change is happening. If the first night is easy the second night will often be more difficult because of this understanding. The third night is where you will start to see definitive improvement.

In the first three days of training, after the 11th hour, depending on how upset your baby is, its ok to stop the training at this hour. Again, this only applies to the first few days of training. We don't want to overwhelm your baby or you, this is a temporary allowance we make in order to keep you motivated. There are three things we are trying to teach your baby: how to go to sleep, how to stay asleep, and how to wake up happy. How to wake up happy is the last step of the training. It is where we address the 11th hour. Early wake ups are the most challenging part of the sleep training process. This is why it is so beneficial to long term sleep skills. This 11th hour will also help with the nap training, since this hour most closely resembles their naps.

After the three days of training, you should see enough progress during the night, to start applying the 15-minute rule, to that 11th hour. Your baby by now should be having long stretches of restorative sleep, she will wake up somewhat rested and happy. Don't rush in, the main purpose of the 15-minute rule is to give your baby a chance to learn patience. From the moment your baby stops "talking" and starts whimpering (does not have to be full on crying) where you see that they're beginning to escalate, start your timer. After 15 minutes, go in. You have three minutes to assess the situation and help them calm slightly. After the three minutes, leave the room. Do another round of 15 minutes. If they're still crying, you can go in and start their day. Ideally, they would maintain their scheduled feeding, even though you're picking them up a little early try to hold off the feeding. We suggest at least one round of the 15-minute rule. Two rounds of 15-minute "patience practice" are ideal. Let the intensity of the crying and your baby's mood determine how many rounds of 15-minute practice you'll do.

When you do decide to start their day, turn on the lights, open the blinds, and start talking to your baby in a happy voice, i.e. "Good morning! What's all this fuss about? You did such a great job!". We want your baby to calm slightly before you pick them up. Show them with nonverbal communication that everything is ok. At this age, their first reaction will be an increase in their crying because they think you're going to leave again. By waiting until your baby calms slightly, you will teach them they do not need to cry in order to get picked up. They will understand that the morning routine means their day is starting and in time, they will smile when you come in. We want to start rewarding positive behaviors.

Things to expect during this phase

Highest likelihood of climbing out of the crib

There is a high likelihood of your baby trying to climb out of their crib, it is ok to go in early if you see them trying to do so. Verbally distract them. If you notice that you're having to go in early more often, or that your baby begins to immediately try to climb out of their crib, it may be time to transfer them to a toddler bed.

Chapter Six

Be prepared to introduce the toddler bed early. Safety is, and should always be, the primary concern. A toddler bed comes with its own challenges, but it is a natural step in your toddler's growth. Sleep training will be a bit tougher but everyone will benefit from the added challenge. Embrace the opportunity!

Frustration leads to temper tantrums

Emotionally, children are very fragile at this age. It is very easy for their frustration to tip over into a full-blown tantrum. At that point, learning stops and they are no longer able to calm themselves. For that reason, parents should absolutely be consistent with the application of the five-minute rule. Frequent resets will keep your toddler from becoming too emotional. Verbal guidance will remind them what they should be doing.

If your child is especially prone to temper tantrums, physical reassurance may be necessary during your resets. Use as needed to make sure that your child doesn't cross the line into tantrum territory. Still limit your resets to keep the focus on them learning to self soothe independently.

7:00 AM – 7:00 PM Schedule

Eighteen to Twenty-Four Months

7:00 – 7:15 AM – Wake up

7:00 – 7:30 AM – First feeding

7:30 AM – 11:00 AM – Activity time

11:00 – 11:30 AM – Second feeding

11:30 – 12:30 PM – Activity time

12:30 – 3:00 PM – Afternoon nap

3:00 – 3:30 PM – Third feeding

3:30 – 6:30 PM – Activity time

6:30 – 7:00 PM – Fourth feeding

7:00 PM – Bedtime

Chapter Six

Babycoach Case Study

Two-year-old Sarah had always been a good sleeper. She was sleep trained by the time she was 12 weeks old. She managed to navigate all of the developmental phases of her first two years while maintaining good sleep habits. At 24 months, the family went on vacation for two weeks where they all had to share a hotel room, this is when the bad habits started being formed.

Due to the unusual environment and worried about disrupting neighbors, Sarah's parents made exemptions at night. They began by extending the nighttime routine, what used to take 30 minutes was now taking upwards of two hours. After the third night, Sarah began asking for her parents to lay with her until she would fall asleep. By the end of the first week, Sarah had begun to wake in the middle of the night crying hysterically and asking for help. Again, she requested they lay with her until she fell asleep. At the end of the vacation, every aspect of Sarah's night had been affected; bedtime, the overnight hours, and her scheduled wake up.

Upon returning home, Sarah's parents expected things to return to normal. It quickly became clear that they wouldn't. Sarah's middle of the night crying escalated into severe tantrums where she would cause herself to vomit. After several instances of this behavior, they started altering her daytime feeding schedule, stopped offering milk at bedtime and started giving her dinner earlier, to try to minimize the amount of food she could spit up at night.

Finally, Sarah's parents had an especially tough time due to Sarah's verbal development. She would often say things like "I need help, please help me" or "mommy please come back". The behaviors continued and began to escalate in frequency over the next two weeks before we were brought in.

How we trained Sarah

We began by reestablishing her normal daytime feeding schedule on the first day. We knew that ultimately it would give Sarah slightly more to spit up during her nighttime tantrums, however training must always be done with a long-term mindset. Since they wanted family dinners to be a normal occurrence, we wanted to establish that from the get go. It ended up serving a dual purpose in that it gave the family a little bit of extra time together just before the nighttime routine which would later provide Sarah with a lot of emotional reassurance.

Our next step was to prepare her parents for the certainty that a spit up event would occur. Since changes are made quickly and decisively during training, Sarah was sure to pick up on them right away. Since spitting up had become a surefire way for her to get her parents to do what she wanted, we knew that she would resort to it. So, we prepared ourselves. Before starting the nighttime routine, we had Sarah's parents set aside several sets of the following into easy access bundles: pajamas, overnight diaper, sheets, and a bedcover. We also had them place cleaning supplies in a very easy to access location within her room. The purpose was to give us the opportunity to quickly change her without needing to search for all of the items, thereby drawing out the process. When the time came for us to change her, we were able to do so within five minutes, where before it had been taking something like 20 minutes.

On the first night of training we had Sarah's parents go through their old nighttime routine. We had them establish certain boundaries with her that they would be able to easily reinforce; i.e. that they would only read two books and that her bath would be 10 minutes. During her bath we had them set a timer. After she was changed and tucked in, they read her exactly two books. Our goal was to help them reestablish trust. We wanted Sarah to understand that her parents would follow through with their words. After the books, we had them give her one last kiss and tell her that they would check on her in five minutes.

Upon her parents leaving the room, Sarah immediately began to cry intensely. We had her parents stand by her closed door ready to respond. Initially, she just stayed in bed crying. After about three minutes we began to see on the monitor that her crying was escalating further. We had her father peek his head in the room to do the first reset. Using a firm tone, he said "Sarah, it's time to go night, night. I'm just checking in. I'll check in again in five minutes." During the first three days of training the exact timing of when her parents went in varied. Since we knew Sarah might spit up at some point, we tried to go in just before she did.

It was during the third round of the five(ish) minute rule, when Sarah made herself spit up. We had her father go in to address it. Since the family had a dimmer installed, we had him turn the lights on the dimmest setting possible. He efficiently changed her while keeping other stimulation to a minimum. Before, they had been giving her a second shower and changing her with the lights fully on. Using wet wipes and quickly changing her clothing and bedding, he managed to be in and out of the room in about six minutes. Just before leaving he verbally reset her, "It's time to go night-night. Daddy loves you and will check on you again in five minutes".

    We saw immediately through the monitor that Sarah was caught off guard. She sat quietly in her bed for a few minutes. Crying resumed but not at the same intensity as before. It took another six rounds of the five-minute rule before she fell asleep. The entire episode lasted about 45 minutes. Due to Sarah's initial bedtime being so physically demanding, she ended up sleeping through the night.

    Sarah tried again the second night. This time, she made herself throw up twice at bedtime. Both times, her father went in and changed her with minimal stimulation. The initial bedtime "event" took slightly longer on the second night, about 70 minutes. It happened again in the middle of the night, because we were prepared our response stayed the same. This second event only took eight minutes. This includes the initial round of the five-minute rule, changing her, and then her eventually putting herself to sleep.

    It was on the third night of training that we began to see Sarah's behavior change. She was still resorting to crying intensely, but the vomiting episodes stopped. We had her parents continue to use the five-

Chapter Six

minute rule. By this point, we could be more consistent in giving her five full minutes before resetting her. It took her 20 minutes at bedtime to fall asleep on her own. We also saw progress on her middle of the night wake up. It only took her three minutes to calm herself and no reset was needed.

On the fourth night of training, we continued to see progress. The intensity of her crying was noticeably diminished, but we continued to have her parents "check in" on her every five minutes. We were still focused on reestablishing trust and wanted to begin reintroducing Sarah's mom into the equation. Sarah managed to fall asleep within ten minutes. Both parents were very encouraged and seemed motivated by her progress. Sarah otherwise slept through the night.

By the fifth night, training was basically done and we shifted into more of a reinforcement mindset. We had her parents continue the five-minute checks. We advised them to continue until she began to fall asleep within five minutes of them initially walking out of the room, which took until night seven. Otherwise, Sarah was sleeping through the night.

We advised her parents to be very consistent with her daytime schedule and nighttime routine for the full two-week reinforcement period.

Chapter Seven

Twenty-Four to Thirty-Six Months

This age is unique in that parents who have trained once before and parents who have never sleep trained their baby are going to face very similar challenges. Consider transitioning your toddler to a toddler bed at 30 months. We find that babies have an easier time transitioning then because they do not yet fully understand the increased freedom that comes with a toddler bed. After 36 months you are likely to find that your baby has a tougher time transitioning and will resist the training.

Before beginning the sleep training process, parents, both those who have trained before and those who haven't, should honestly assess whether their toddler is ready for a toddler bed. If your toddler shows any signs of trying to climb out of their crib, you should seriously consider making the change now during training. You don't want to train your baby in their crib only to have to retrain them in a few months because of the toddler bed. We know how scary it can be!

How to sleep train at this age

Baby is healthy

If your toddler is in some sort of daycare, daytime class, or nursery school, frequent illness is very common. It is possible to sleep train them if they're exhibiting mild symptoms such as a runny nose, cough, or sneezing. If your baby was sick at one point and still has lingering symptoms but seems otherwise healthy, you can begin the sleep training process.

Keep your pediatrician up to date with your plans. Trust your assessment that your toddler is well enough to go through the process. If your toddler is showing more serious signs of an illness or that they're about to become ill, such as fever, lack of appetite, or vomiting, hold off on training until they're healthy.

Baby is safe

If you have decided to transition to the toddler bed, reassess your toddler's nursery entirely. Baby proof the nursery if you haven't already. Drawer stops, electrical socket covers, door handles; anything that can become a safety issue, will become a safety issue. Try to see your toddler's nursery through their eyes. Any loose cords should be moved out of reach or tucked away behind furniture

Depending on your toddler's personality, furniture can also become a safety hazard. Toddlers can climb bookshelves, side tables, chairs, etc. If they show any signs of climbing behavior, use furniture safety anchors to prevent pieces from toppling over. Try to be a step ahead if possible.

Be conscious of the placement of your toddler's nursery furniture. Any stools or chairs in your toddler's nursery can be used to turn on their bedroom lights or open their doors. Furniture should be moved so that they cannot be used to achieve a separate goal. Your toddler will be highly motivated during training. We've seen children use stools to gain the height needed to climb over baby gates, use step stools to pull door handles, etc.

Baby is in an environment conducive to sleep

Toddler's this age benefit from having a nightlight. The light should be placed behind a piece of furniture, so that the light is diffused. Be conscious of how bright the nightlight is. Choose a dimmer or warmer light if possible. The aim of the light is to provide just enough light for them to see shapes and objects but not so much light that they can see specific details of their room. The best way to assess how bright their room really is, is to spend some time there after they fall asleep

Lullabies with lyrics are preferred since your toddler is expanding their vocabulary. You can also use audiobooks or a recording of you reading books if that is more to your liking. If your baby is being exposed to a second or third language, this is a great time to use those languages. A recording of your own voice reading or reciting books, letters, numbers, etc. can all be used. As long as you use an even steady rhythm and a calm tone, the recording will be effective. We want to use their curiosity towards speech to help distract them if they begin to cry overnight. The volume should be slightly lower, enough that they are motivated to quiet in order to hear what is being said.

Finally, to help your toddler with the early morning hours, you can use a timer on a specific light or a "wake up" clock. Tell your child that they can call for you when the light turns on or the clock changes color, usually red to green. There are some truly wonderful products to help signal your toddler when they can begin their day. Keep it simple. A clock that changes color or lights up at a certain time is all that is needed. If they cry in the middle of the night or cry out for you, reset them by reminding them to wait for the light.

Baby is in an emotional place where they can learn

Use the five-minute rule to sleep train your toddler. It's important that parents understand that going in to reset their toddler is the best possible thing they can do at this age. Due to the fact that the habits created have been reinforced for so long, establishing trust will be one of the main goals of the sleep training process. By going in to reset them at a regular interval, you are showing through your actions that they are not going to get the result they want. This repeated reminder is what will ultimately get you the results you're after and will teach them that you mean what you say.

A staple of this age is your child noticing that a change is occurring and changing their behavior to try to bring back the old habits. You may notice that they begin trying to negotiate or make specific requests whenever you enter the room to reset them, i.e. "I need water", "I need to go potty", or "I'm scared". As training progresses, they may stop trying to negotiate (when they notice it's not working) and further change their behavior. They may start trying to exit their room quietly without you noticing, may start kicking their door, throwing stuffed animals or toys, trying to bang their heads or limbs on hard surfaces, etc. The point here, is that they will notice very clearly that your behavior is changing and they will try to test your resolve in many different ways. Be prepared for anything and stay consistent throughout. It will be your consistency that shows your child that this is the new way of things and that they will only get positive reinforcement one way, cooperation.

Verbal communication should be your primary tool during sleep training. While your child may want physical reassurance, verbal communication will help to establish boundaries and will kickstart them developing their own self soothing skills more easily. Whenever you need to reset your toddler, keep your directions clear and to the point. You're telling your child what to do, reminding them what they should be focused on. What you say should be determined by what they're currently doing. For instance, if they're out of bed, you can say "Get back in bed, it's time to go night, night". If they managed to stay in their bed, say "Good job staying in bed, go night- night". You can also use this time to continually remind them that you'll be checking on them again. At the end of every reset say "I'll check on you again in five minutes". Just as, if not more, important than what you say is how you say it. A firm tone should always be used. You're not pleading or trying to cajole them; you're telling your child what to do. Be firm, so that they understand you mean it.

Overall, resets at this age should not last very long at all. While you can still reset them for the full three minutes, aim to stay in their room as little as you possibly can. This will keep the focus on them learning to self soothe independently.

Expect that the initial bedtime episode, i.e. them managing to put themselves to sleep, will take anywhere between 60 to 120 minutes. This is due to habits being more deeply ingrained and your toddler's increased ability to understand that their behavior gets a certain response. Middle of the night wake ups should take about half as long as whatever it took during the first episode, if it took your toddler 60 minutes to fall asleep expect middle of the night episodes to take about 30 minutes.

Chapter Seven

The first night will be your baseline and will help you measure your baby's progress. The five-minute rule should be used until the 11th hour. At that point you will want to begin using the 15-minute rule. Ideally you will do at least two rounds of the 15-minute rule before beginning your baby's day. Their scheduled feeding time shouldn't change if you decide to pick them up early.

You should see significant improvement nightly as your baby practices. If the first night of training is fairly easy, prepare yourself for the second night, this is supposed to be challenging. By this age your baby should understand that change is happening and be more difficult because of this understanding. The third night is where you should start to see definitive improvement.

In the first three days of training, after the 11th hour, depending on how upset your baby is, its ok to stop the training at this hour. Again, this only applies for the first few days of training. We don't want to overwhelm your baby or you so this is a temporary allowance that we make in order to keep you motivated. There are three things we are trying to teach your baby: how to go to sleep, how to stay asleep, and how to wake up happy. How to wake up happy is the last step of the training. It is where we address the 11th hour. Early wake ups are the most challenging part of the sleep training process. This is why it is so beneficial to long term sleep skills. This 11th hour will also help with the nap training, since this hour most closely resembles their naps.

After the three days of training, you should see enough progress during the night, to start applying the

15-minute rule, to that 11th hour. By now, they should be having long stretches of restorative sleep, she will wake up somewhat rested and happy. Don't rush in, the main purpose of the 15-minute rule is to give them a chance to learn patience. From the moment your they stop "talking" and starts whimpering (does not have to be full on crying) where you see that they're beginning to escalate, start your timer. After 15 minutes, go in. You have three minutes to assess the situation and help them calm slightly. After the three minutes, leave the room. Do another round of 15 minutes. If they're still crying, you can go in and start their day. Maintain their scheduled feeding. Picking them up early is an exception and the feeding is the rule, so it should stay consistent. We suggest at least one round of the 15-minute rule. Two rounds of 15-minute "patience practice" are ideal. Let the intensity of the crying and their mood determine how many rounds of 15-minute practice you'll do.

When you do decide to start their day, turn on the lights, open the blinds, and start talking to them in a happy voice, i.e. "Good morning! What's all this fuss about? You did such a great job!". We want them to calm slightly before you pick them up. Show them with nonverbal communication that everything is ok. At this age, their first reaction will be an increase in their crying because they think you're going to leave again. By waiting until they calm slightly, you will teach them they do not need to cry in order to get picked up. They will understand that the morning routine means their day is starting and in time, they will smile when you come in. We want to start rewarding positive behaviors.

Chapter Seven

Things to expect during this phase

Resists change in routine

This age is marked by a staunch resistance to change. Your toddler can't help their impulses. Sleep training is about learning self-soothing skills. Parents need to understand this tendency to have knee jerk impulses in their child, in order to make allowances for them, while moving toward our goal of independent sleep. When you stop responding in a way your toddler is accustomed to, parents need to be ready for new behaviors.

An increased level of frustration is a strong motivator. You may find that things get "worse" with your toddler once training begins. This clash is between your toddler's resolve to keep things as they are and your resolve to change your circumstances. Both of you are trying to train (or retrain in your toddler's case) the other.

If your toddler is especially close/reliant on one parent over the other than the other parent should take the lead during the first few days of training as this will make the training process easier on both toddler and parent.

Start developing auditory fears

At this age, your toddler may begin to show signs of fears. Always provide reassurance but try not feed the fear. There is nothing for your toddler to be afraid of.

Using soothing sounds or lullabies is something we suggest at all ages, but it is especially useful at this developmental stage. We strongly recommend parents consider using some sort of sound related soothing tool to help prevent these fears from developing. The lullabies, melodic sounds, will keep their minds occupied with a soothing distraction.

Uses language to resist and defy. Attempts to bargain with adults

Toddlers will try to engage in conversation during resets. They may try to tell you why they can't or won't do what you're telling them to do. Do not engage. If it is a practical request (for instance bathroom) then you can accommodate that request twice, since they may have an actual need. Imposing that hard limit on yourself will help you to stick with the training and eliminate your own fears of ignoring their needs.

Anything can become a negotiation tactic ("I'm afraid", "I'm thirsty", "I'm scared"). Be thoughtful of your response. You will know when the purpose of the request is to prolong the nighttime routine, at that point you should start saying no. Part of teaching them to become an independent sleeper is to have expectations of them knowing that those expectations are reasonable and can be met.

Chapter Seven

Change to toddler bed

One of the most difficult aspects of this developmental phase is the adjustment to the increased freedom a toddler has, once they begin to use a toddler bed. Make peace with the fact that you cannot make your toddler stay in bed. You can and should set rules (toddler can read in bed, wait for the timed light to turn on before leaving bed, etc.) but you will have to make concessions. Pick your battles.

Development will always come with an irresistible pull to try new things. We often try to remind parents that as infants a child's safe space is their crib, as toddlers it's their room, and as teenagers it's their home. That is a person's natural development. Your child will just become more independent over time. It's your job as a parent to know when your child is ready and to let them have the freedom to try. Imposing boundaries is key, as long as they're safe in their room that's a victory for you.

7:00 AM – 7:00 PM Schedule

Twenty-Four to Thirty-Six Months

7:00 – 7:15 AM – Wake up

7:00 – 7:30 AM – First feeding

7:30 –11:00 AM – Activity time

11:00 – 11:30 AM – Second feeding

11:30 – 1:00 PM – Activity time

1:00 – 3:00 PM – Afternoon nap

3:00 – 3:30 PM – Third feeding

3:30 – 6:00 PM – Activity time

6:00 – 6:30 PM – Dinner with family

6:30 – 7:00 PM – Fourth feeding

7:00 PM – Bedtime

Chapter Seven

Babycoach Case Study

Rosie was an outspoken, cheerful, and vibrant 2.5-year-old. When her parents, Bill and Camille, first reached out to us they let us know that she was an expert in how to push their buttons and get her way. She never really learned to sleep through the night. Normally she would sleep six to eight hours but would occasionally sleep nine to ten hours. She and her seven-year-old brother Matt would frequently end up sleeping in Bill and Camille's room. Camille contacted us after her final attempt at sleep training Rosie resulted in her throwing all of her toys out of the room and learning to climb the gate that was newly installed. Camille used a more disciplinarian approach that had Rosie reacting in defiance. The final straw was Rosie learning to climb the curtains and nearly injuring herself when she climbed too high.

How we trained Rosie

Our entire approach was designed around shifting the family dynamic from one of confrontation/discipline to one of cooperation. Our first priority was to ensure Rosie's safety during the sleep training process. We first had Bill temporarily remove the curtains so that she wouldn't be able to climb when upset. We also removed the gate to further discourage her climbing.

Our first step with Rosie, was to prepare her by explaining why we were there. We involved her in the process by letting her have a say in what toys would be kept in the room and by asking her if she'd like the door closed or slightly open. We made it clear that these choices were made to help her stay in bed.

We involved her older brother Matt in the process as well. Since he was also struggling to stay in bed at night, we wanted to use their close relationship to their advantage. We added a light up clock to both of their rooms. We then gave Matt the "job" of helping her start her day when the clock lit up. Being seven at the time, we explained his job in a way that empowered him and emphasized how much she needed his "big brother" help. We made it very clear to both children what their jobs were. Rosie's job was to sleep until the clock lit up or until Matt came to get her. Matt's job was to sleep until the clock let him know that it was okay to help Rosie.

Part of this tactic was explaining to Bill and Camille that they needed to relax their expectations of how Matt and Rosie would start their day. By the end of the training they started to see a pattern of quiet morning playtime and reading emerge that they could appreciate while working towards our ultimate goal of having Rosie sleep twelve hours.

The first two nights of the training required frequent resets of both Rosie and Matt. We focused on reminding them of their clocks. Rosie tried to exit her room several times both nights. After three resets, we began to close her door since it wasn't helping her to stay in bed. We used that as a privilege she could earn back by staying in her bed. By the third night of training, she understood and was able to stay in her bed after just a reset or two. This behavior was completely gone by the fifth night of training.

The key to this training ended up being Matt and his morning "job". Once Rosie realized that she would get to see her brother first thing in the morning and play together before breakfast, she became an eager and active participant in the sleep training process. It became clear after the third night of training that both children flourished, the sense of cooperation brought a sense of pride and the added sleep made the entire process that much easier. Bill and Camille were thrilled with the lessons learned and the consistency of the routine made their days more manageable.

We ended the process with a two-week reinforcement period where the family daytime routine was kept consistent.

Chapter Eight

Three to Five Years

If your child has been previously trained, you should find that retraining at this age will be easy to do. It will come down to how consistently a parent reinforces the changes and rules they put in place. Open communication will go a long way to making this process easier. Keep in mind your parenting behavior during the day will reflect on your child's nights. You cannot expect them to respond well and follow rules just at bedtime. If at any point you feel that your child's sleep is not quite where you want it to be, revert to the four basics.

If you've never sleep trained your child. It is important to accept that at this point training is entirely behavior modification, for both of you. Your child has become accustomed to getting what they want, and you have become accustomed to finding a justification to give them what they want. For your child to truly become an independent sleeper, both will have to change.

How to sleep train at this age

Child is healthy

Before beginning, make sure they are healthy. Parents should try to sleep train when their child is on summer vacation or an extended school break.

Child is safe

By now your child should be in a full bed. Since you can verbally communicate with them, you will be able to tell them what is and is not safe. That should make the whole process safer overall. Two days before you begin sleep training, start telling them what you plan to do. (i.e. "Starting Friday, Mommy is going to help you learn to sleep in your own bed"). Communicate in their own unique way to try to help them understand what is ahead and what will be expected of them.

Chapter Eight
Child is in an environment conducive to sleep.

At this age, a very soft nightlight may make them more comfortable during the overnight hours. If they request lighter, you may offer them a small flashlight. The flashlight is a privilege that your child may keep and use if they meet that expectation, i.e. staying in bed and sleeping all night. Don't use taking the flashlight away as a punishment. Present withholding the privilege as a way to help them, rather than a punishment. For instance, if your child has a flashlight but keeps getting out of bed you can say "Would it help you stay in bed if Daddy took the flashlight?" Chances are they will immediately say no. Respond with "Ok. So, you must stay in bed with your flashlight".

You will have to make some concessions to help your child navigate the overnight hours. This may include extra books near their bed, more than one stuffed animal in bed, etc. Electronic devices (tablets, phones, etc.), should stay out of the room they sleep in, as they are too stimulating and will interfere with sleep.

If you've never used soothing sounds of lullabies, they won't be as effective as a soothing tool at this point. You may consider audiobooks that will continue to play for 30-45 minutes after you've left the room. Again, this is also a privilege that should be turned off after three warnings, i.e. if your child has gotten out of bed, the privilege of the audio book is withheld.

Finally, you can introduce a light up clock or other alarm clock that will let them know when it is ok for them to get out of bed. Make sure to include your child in the set-up process and explain to them how the clock will help them.

Child is in an emotional place where they can learn

Maintain as much as possible of their current routine. Since they are comfortable and familiar with it, this will help make the sleep training process less jarring. The only thing that should change is whatever behavior you want to eliminate, i.e. having to lay in bed with your child, too many books, nighttime routine that drags on, etc.

Start the training a few days ahead by communicating with your child that they're going to learn how to sleep by themselves. This should only occur two to three days before you're set to begin training. It's enough time to give them a chance to emotionally prepare for the change, but not so long that they're able to become anxious about it.

Once you're ready to start training, go through your nighttime routine. Here is where you can begin to make changes. If the main problem you're trying to change is that the nighttime routine takes too long, start streamlining it. Communicate these new limits and stick with them. If you say bath time will only take ten minutes, set a timer and stick with it. If you'll only read three books, only read three books. Your child will try to test your resolve, so be prepared to reinforce the new boundaries. This will be key to the overall process, since one of the main goals of sleep training at this age is to teach them to trust you. You mean what you say and your actions will reinforce your words.

End your nighttime routine by saying "Good night, I love you. I'll check on you in a few minutes." Here is when they are likely to start crying. Guide them to listen to their audiobook, comfort them with the reassurance that you will check back in two minutes. Be encouraging but firm. Exit the room in a timely fashion.

Stand right outside their door with the monitor (on silent) and observe their behavior. Ideally, you'll wait outside their room for two minutes before resetting them. Base how long it takes to reset them on their behavior. If you see that they are trying to stay calm, give them two full minutes. If you see that they're about to hop out of bed or that their behavior is escalating, you can reset them sooner.

When the time comes, open their door and verbally reset them. What you say should be determined by their behavior. If they've gotten out of bed, say "get back in bed. It's time to go to sleep. I love you.". If they've stayed in bed, say "good job staying in bed. I love you, go to sleep.". Remember to use a firm, steady tone. Do not engage in verbal negotiation or try to coax your child to sleep. Your tone will let them know that you are in charge. End your reset by saying "I'll check on you in a few minutes". Close their door and repeat.

Children with stronger personalities may need to be physically reset on occasion. Be mindful, that they can quickly learn that their behavior can gain them further attention from you, so use these physical resets sparingly. If you find that your child's behavior escalates as you're verbally resetting them or that they have gotten out of bed entirely you should physically reset them. Guide them back to bed and tuck them in. Don't linger any longer than necessary. Remind them to stay in bed and that you'll check on them again in a few minutes. Exit the room, even if they immediately try to follow you. Hold their door closed while you wait to reset them.

Repeat the frequent "check ins" until they fall asleep. The average 3-year-old will take anywhere from 1 to 1.5 hours to initially fall asleep. Learning how to fall asleep independently will naturally help them learn to fall back asleep if and when they wake in the night. Chances are they will sleep fairly well for the rest of the night, since they used so much energy initially falling asleep.

Regardless, now your focus should shift to the middle of the night. Again, during the first night of training, it's unlikely that they will wake up frequently in the middle of the night. This is much more likely to happen during the second, third, and fourth nights of training. During those nights, they will still resist at bedtime but will have more energy to resist throughout the night so be prepared. How you prepare should be based on your child's previous behavior and their personality. Think of this as a chess match, you need to predict their behavior and have a response ready beforehand.

Chapter Eight
Common child behaviors and possible responses

Open their bedroom door to call out

    Install babyproof device on door knob

    Install child gate

    Turn off or dim hallway lights

Sneak into parent's bed

    Install a child gate

    Lock parents' door

    Install babyproof device on door knobs

Turns on bedroom lights to prevent sleep

    Install babyproof device on light switch

    Install smart plug on light

    Move furniture so that they can't reach

Children at this age are prone to knee jerk reactions, they don't always consciously think before acting. Preparing beforehand will allow you to get ahead of these knee jerk reactions and leave them with no choice but to call out for you. Here again, your preparation will pay off because you will be able to wake up and correct their behavior instead of falling back on old habits due to exhaustion. Be creative and adjust as you go since you may find that your little one gets creative themselves when they see your new response. When you do find yourself having to reset them in the middle of the night your response should be the same as it was at bedtime. Guide them back to their room or bed and verbally guide them. Check in steadily and verbally reset them as needed until they fall back to sleep. Repeat throughout the night.

As they begin to trust your check ins, you can start lengthening the time between checks to the full five minutes. This way they're more likely to fall asleep and you still get to show them that you will keep your word. It will take time to work your way up, but be patient they will get there. Resist the temptation to speed the process along or to take short cuts. Make the most of the learning process by being patient. Let them learn at their own pace. That is how you get long term results, that they will always be able to fall back on.

The early morning hours are often the toughest for children and parents to master. The increased difficulty of these hours, the last two especially, is what makes them so important to long term success. You can make exceptions during the first two to three nights of training and decide to start their days early. Once you start to see them make progress, it's time to start taking those hours more seriously. Use the five-minute rule consistently until the 11th hour. As you get closer to their scheduled wake up, make sure to remind them to wait for their clock to light up or change color. Really emphasize this physical cue so that they learn to focus on it and appreciate its importance. During the 11th hour, your approach should be the same while using the 15-minute patience practice rule instead of the five-minute rule.

When the time comes, be prepared to offer a lot of praise and congratulations, even if they struggled through the night. Tell them how proud you are and can offer them a favorite breakfast as a reward or extra cuddles throughout the day. If they really struggled, reassure them. Let them know how proud you are that they tried and that you'll both try again that night. Keep your day as normal and uneventful as possible.

Prepare for the second night. While children tend to do better, it is not uncommon for the second night to be more difficult than the first. This is especially true if the first night went well. By this age, they will be able to realize that these changes are here to stay. They will come to that realization, over time with your consistent response. Stand firm. Be consistent. You should begin to see noticeable improvement by the third night. Every night after should also show improvement.

Things to expect during this phase

Dramatic and dogmatic

This age is marked by dramatic and dogmatic behavior. Be ready for over the top reactions. Any deeply set habits will be difficult to change since children will actively resist changes. Stay cool and calm. This is normal.

If you don't reward the behavior, children are less likely to use it. Your response will always determine your child's behavior. Be their rock during their dramatics, resist the pull.

Urge to conform/please is diminished

Again, sleep training at this point is behavior modification. Your children will be less compliant and flexible. Do not be discouraged since this will only make starting the training process more difficult over time as they get older.

May exhibit control issues

Since children may exhibit control issues at this age, try to stay a step ahead. Close their door during the nighttime routine. This will give you a chance to exit their room before they can climb out of bed and reach the door. This will also give you a chance to execute the sleep training plan.

The same philosophy should be utilized in other areas. If your child immediately turns on their bedroom light, you should take steps to keep that from happening. Be ready beforehand and be ready to adapt your response along the way.

May be physically aggressive

If your child becomes physically aggressive, you should contain them until they regain a sense of calm. Your goal should be to keep them from harming you or

Chapter Eight

themselves. Physical aggression must always be addressed.

Use short sentences, i.e. "No! We don't hit!", with a very firm tone. Be gentle and in control, children learn more from what you do, than what you say. Consistency will be absolutely key to discouraging physical aggression overall.

Nightmares

Although nightmares may occur, parents should make sure that the claims of being scared are followed by physical symptoms of fear, such as cold sweat, increased pulse, or dilated pupils. If that is the case, reassure them. Children notice, early that the claim of being scared, gets an immediate reaction from their parents. You can show them the video monitor to remind them that you're always making sure that they're safe.

When it comes to nightmares, all you can do is to support your child until they stop occurring. At the same time, we do not want to reward or reinforce the fear by laying with them or having them sleep in your bed. Nightmares tend to become more frequent and last longer when they're rewarded this way, as the lines of a real episode of nightmare and the attention they get if they claim fear gets blurry. Just be mindful, you must acknowledge and be sensitive towards their fears or confusion while not catering to them.

Children at this age are very perceptive and will pick up your own fear and anxiety, be warned that children can learn to say that they're scared or afraid even if they're not actually currently feeling that way. Verbal manipulation is very common.

Uses bathroom unassisted (4 years old)

If you're starting to potty train at night, we suggest that you remind your child to go to the bathroom just before bed. Just before you go to bed, three to four hours after your child goes to bed, go to their room and wake them for a potty break. Use your words "Let's go potty" so that they begin to associate waking in the middle of the night with going to the bathroom.

Check their pull up during this scheduled wake up. If it's wet, try to cut their liquid in take one hour before bedtime, allowing only small sips of water during that last hour. You can also wake them a little earlier for the potty break. You want to find the window just before they use the pull up so they actually go potty during this scheduled wake up. If the pull up is wet, you should exchange it for a new one. This will allow you to monitor it for the remainder of your child's night. Repeat for three nights or until the first pull up is dry at the bedtime potty break. This dry pull up will occur once you find the right amount of liquid to give you child before bedtime.

Once you wake them up and the pull up is dry and your child actually uses the bathroom, you should begin to monitor how that scheduled wake up affects the pull up in the early morning hours. If it's still wet, you'll have to schedule another potty break between your bedtime and your child's scheduled wake up. Once they

Chapter Eight

no longer wet their pull ups for a week, you can begin overnight potty training.

A nightlight should be added to your child's bathroom or the shared bathroom to be used. Wake them with minimal talking, they should know what to do at this point. Allow them to go to the bathroom without your assistance. Practice with you supervising and them going to the bathroom independently, for a week. If they are doing well, allow them to try one night on their own. You will have some accidents, but they should be old enough to learn quickly how to do it by themselves. By this point, they will have gotten used to sleeping with a dry pull up, they will notice if they sleep through a bathroom break.

7:00 AM – 7:00 PM Schedule

Three to Five Years

7:00 – 7:15 AM – Wake up

7:00 – 7:30 AM – First feeding

7:30 – 11:00 AM – Activity time

11:00 – 11:30 AM – Second feeding

11:30 – 1:00 PM – Activity time

1:00 – 3:00 PM – Afternoon nap

3:00 – 3:30 PM – Third feeding

3:30 – 6:00 PM – Activity time

6:00 – 6:30 PM – Dinner with family

6:30 – 7:00 PM – Nighttime routine

7:00 PM – Bedtime

Chapter Eight
Babycoach case study

Julie started to sleep through the night by the time she was 10 weeks old. She was nap trained by the time she was 14 weeks old. She navigated every potential sleep set back that can occur through the first year, with ease.

The family dynamic changed when she was 18 months and her parents started living separately. Now with two different households, the parents found themselves giving in to her emotional out bursts as they too were learning how to navigate the changes. Eventually one parent found themselves allowing her to sleep in their room. The other parent bought Julie a larger bed so that they could sleep in her room with her. Julie began to go to sleep later and wake up earlier which led to her being grumpier than usual during the day. With life now settled, the family was left with a three-year-old strong-willed little girl that didn't sleep well, even with all the concessions her parents have made.

How we sleep trained Julie

Our main goal during this training was to reset the boundaries between Julie and her parents. First, we found that a way to motivate and ease the transition was to rearrange her nursery into more of a "bigger kid" room. The idea was to establish a clear point of reset.

We also chose to introduce music, as Julie likes to sing and listen to music during her rides to and from school. We gave her some input to make sure the songs chosen were ones she liked. We made sure to limit her choices to slower, less stimulating, songs.

We also decided to add a soft night light as one of reasons she gave for not wanting to sleep in her room was fear. Again, we gave her some input so she could feel empowered by the sleep training process.

Finally, we installed a timer on her side table lamp that would let her know when it was time to call for mommy or daddy.

We started Julie's training on a Thursday night, before a long holiday weekend. This gave us four nights where we did not have to worry about Julie being too tired for school. It drastically cut down of both parents' stress levels and made them more confident in the process. It was agreed that both were ready and willing to reinforce the routine in both households.

The first night, as expected, was filled with a lot of negotiating and heart wrenching pleas. We had her mother go in every three minutes to reset her emotionally. We had her repeat short sentences, making it clear what she expected from her. We also reminded her that she was in her big girl room, she was going to have beautiful dreams and that she could get mom when her light went on. Initially it took her just over 50 minutes to fall asleep. She ended up sleeping through the night.

The second and third nights showed great improvement in her initial bedtime. We saw much less negotiating and she was quicker to comply when given direct reminders. We did see new behaviors, which we were expecting. She had started sleeping with more than one stuffed animal and started whispering to them before falling asleep. It was an adjustment for her parents, since they wanted her to immediately fall asleep like she used to. We saw this as an overall positive behavior.

We did have to reinforce the training during the day, since Julie had such a strong personality. We recommended that both parents start enforcing their rules consistently during the day so that we could send a consistent and united message. It was very important, in this case, for both parents to work together so that she could have the same rules, or at least similar ones, at both households.

Julie showed steady improvement throughout the training period. However, again due to her strong personality and the dual households, she needed a longer reinforcement period. Every few nights, especially when she changed households, she would test the boundaries to see if her parents would remain consistent. This boundary testing behavior remained through the entire two-week reinforcement period. In fact, it took about a month for her to become truly consistent.

Chapter Eight

Chapter Nine

5 years and Beyond

Children of this age usually welcome the opportunity to develop a greater sense of independence. If your child has not yet developed the skills necessary to be an independent sleeper, chances are that you will notice that during the day their sense of independence has been affected.

In our experience, children that sleep with their parents or rely on parental/adult support at night have a greater need for emotional support in all areas of their daily life. This often translates to a reluctance to play alone, constant need to be entertained by an adult, greater chances of emotional episodes, "meltdowns", difficulty making friends, and an overall difficulty socializing with people they're unfamiliar with (distant family members, neighbors).

If you've picked up this book, you've realized that whatever you've been doing has not brought you the positive results you want for your family. We don't point these things out to judge you. We know that these habits were formed with the best of intentions. We know how easily these habits were developed. We just want parents to realize that sleep training at this age requires a change not just at night but during the day as well.

Encouraging your child's sense of independence must be a primary parenting goal. Think of it this way, your child's emotional self needs to be exposed to new challenges in order to become stronger. Becoming emotionally independent to some extent, is what will help your child learn to play independently, be more emotionally even keeled, and help develop their social skills.

You can try encouraging them to play alone for a few minutes while you make lunch, go to the bathroom without supervision, choose their own outfit for the day. Take advantage of every opportunity to encourage independence and you'll soon see that they'll start seeking these opportunities for themselves.

If your child has been sleep trained in the past, you do have a significant advantage both emotionally and psychologically. They know that they were able to sleep through the night independently and so do you. If you've never trained your child this age is actually a great time to do so, the only comparing phase is 12 weeks. Naturally children will want to assert their independence, you should notice that they will not only cooperate but want to go at a faster pace. Another advantage is that the remaining nap (if it still exists) is no longer necessary. This increased activity time and reduced sleep will result in an overall easier bedtime.

Chapter Nine

On the other hand, this is one of the tougher times for parents to sleep train, since the child's dependence has its own emotional reward. We cannot reiterate enough; patterns of behavior go both ways. Five years of a conditioned response takes real effort to overcome. For that reason, the parents become the deciding factor of whether training will be successful. The knee jerk responses that you will have grown used to will be difficult to break, but it can be done.

Take this training period, to train yourself. Focus some of your efforts on an activity that you otherwise couldn't do pre-training. This can be anything from exercising, dinner with your spouse/partner or other adult, enjoying a book with some wine, anything really. The main goal is to do something exclusively for yourself that you find fulfilling that will take the place of the fulfillment you received by helping your child.

How to sleep train at this age

Child is healthy

To begin this process, they must be healthy. They should not be showing any symptoms of illness. At the same time, consider where they are emotionally. You don't want to begin sleep training the week before they are to start school, go on vacation, etc. You will need a minimum of two weeks of steady reinforcement after the training period. Any new activities or life events should occur after this period, so try to plan accordingly. The more consistent their daily schedule, the better.

Child is safe

Take your child's personality into account. At this age, children have a better understanding of risk and danger so things like pulling shelves, climbing dressers. becomes less likely to occur.

The main thing parents should be concerned with is trying to circumvent your child's conditioned response. If, for instance, your child wakes up in the middle of the night and immediately leaves their bed to go to your room. Put some sort of barrier in place that will stop them and cause them to call out for you. The barrier is up to you, it can be a gate at your child's door, locking the door to *your* room, putting a chair in front of your door, whatever you are comfortable with. The main goal of this barrier is to wake you so that you can correct your child's behavior. You don't want to wake up in the morning and realize that you don't know when your child snuck into your room. You want the chance to reset the behavior so that learning can occur.

Use your child's current and past behavior and try to prepare as much as you can before training begins. Be prepared to adjust as the training progress, since it is fairly common to see children exhibit new behaviors due to new parental responses.

Child is in an environment conducive to sleep

Before beginning the training process, consider introducing an alarm clock with numbers. It's a great option that will give your child a clear understanding of what is expected from them and will be something you can remind them of during the night. This clock will let them know when its ok to get out of bed or call out for you.

Also consider having a nightlight in their bathroom so that they can use the bathroom if/when necessary. A nightlight can also be used in their bedroom, just not within their direct line of sight. Place it behind a piece of furniture so that the light can be diffused. Generally, we recommend the darkest environment possible since it results in the most restorative sleep.

Child is in an emotional place where they can learn

Before you start the process of changing a behavior and training your child to sleep independently, remind yourself of how long you have reinforced these patterns. The longer a child has been exposed to and had a behavior reinforced, the longer it will take to establish a new one. This will be directly tied to how much resistance parents should expect and how much crying they will exhibit. We are not trying to be discouraging. The result will be more than worth the effort. We simply want parents to be prepared for the worst, so that their resolve will be able to carry them through long enough to achieve positive results. You didn't get here in one night. Good sleep habits take time and are the result of consistent effort over time. Stay calm and be patient.

Since your child has a wide vocabulary and greater awareness of the world, the first thing you should do is to prepare them beforehand. Tell them when training will begin and what you will be expecting of them. Put their mind at rest that they can do it. Be clear with your words. Your tone is just as important as what you're saying. If you're dreading the experience your child will pick up on it! It is important that you project confidence. This will give them time to understand the changes that are coming and be part of the preparation for those changes.

While it is not a necessary step, a physical change to their environment will give them a clear visual understanding that things are changing and will physically reinforce your words. Rearrange their room. Buy new books or sheets. Make them a special blanket. Add a special clock or light that will let them know when they can get out of bed. Be creative.

Try to listen as well, address any questions they might have. It is important that your child feels heard. If you are faced with questions of fear or a sense of anxiety, reassure them that you will be there to help them. Use phrases such as "I understand, we will be there to help you through it" or "you're safe in your room, at home, with us". This conversation should occur a couple days before the training is set to begin and it should be brought up occasionally until the training starts.

Once you're ready to start training, go through your nighttime routine. Here is where you can begin to make changes. If the main problem you're try to change is that the nighttime routine takes to too long, start streamlining it. Communicate these new limits and stick with them. If you say bath time will only take ten minutes, set a timer and stick with it. If you'll only read three books, only read three books. Your child will try to test your resolve, so be prepared to reinforce the new boundaries. This will be key to the overall process, since one of the main goals of sleep training at this age is to teach them to trust you. You mean what you say and your actions will reinforce your words.

End your nighttime routine by saying "Good night, I love you. I'll check on you in a few minutes." Here is when they are likely to start crying. Guide them to listen to their audiobook, you can also offer a flash light that would allow them to read a couple of more books, without you being in the room, comfort them with the reassurance that you will check back in two minutes. Be encouraging but firm. Exit the room in a timely fashion.

Start training with their door closed. Since their habits are so deeply engrained, an open door is almost too much temptation. Closing their door increases their chances of success especially the first few nights. Keeping the door open is a privilege they can earn by staying in their bed. Once they start to consistently stay in their bed, you can start leaving the door cracked open. Leaving the door completely open should only happen when they've shown that they're able to resist the temptation it presents entirely. If it any time, you see that they're sliding back to old habits start closing the door again.

Stand right outside their door with the monitor (on silent) and observe their behavior. Ideally, you'll wait outside their room for two minutes before resetting them. Base how long it takes to reset them on their behavior. If you see that your toddler is trying to stay calm, give them two full minutes. If you see that they're about to hop out of bed or that their behavior is escalating, you can reset them sooner.

When the time comes, open their door and verbally reset them. What you say should be determined by their behavior. If they've gotten out of bed, say "get back in bed. It's time to go to sleep. I love you.". If they've stayed in bed, say "good job staying in bed. I love you, go to sleep.". Remember to use a firm, steady tone. Do not engage in verbal negotiation or try to coax your child to sleep. Your tone will let them know that you are in charge. End your reset by saying "I'll check on you in a few minutes". Close their door and repeat.

Children with stronger personalities may need to be physically reset on occasion. Be mindful, that they can quickly learn that their behavior can gain them further attention from you, so use these physical resets sparingly. If you find that your child's behavior escalates as you're verbally resetting them or that they have gotten out of bed entirely you should physically reset them. Guide them back to bed and tuck them in. Don't linger any longer than necessary. Remind them to stay in bed and that you'll check on them again in a few minutes. Exit the room, even if they immediately try to follow you. Hold their door closed while you wait to reset them.

Repeat the frequent "check ins" until they fall asleep. The average 5-year-old will take anywhere from one to two hours to initially fall asleep. Learning how to fall asleep independently will naturally help them learn to fall back asleep if and when they wake in the night. Chances are they will sleep fairly well for the rest of the night, since they used so much energy initially falling asleep.

Regardless, now your focus should shift to the middle of the night. Again, during the first night of training, it's unlikely that they will wake up frequently in the middle of the night. This is much more likely to happen during the second, third, and fourth nights of training. During those nights, they will still resist at bedtime but will have more energy to resist throughout the night so be prepared. How you prepare should be based on your child's previous behavior and their personality. Think of this as a chess match, you need to predict their behavior and have a response ready beforehand.

Chapter Nine

Common child behaviors and possible responses

Sneak a tablet for entertainment

    Install parental locks to limit use

    Remove the tablet when exiting their room

    Disable WIFI

Frequently wakes and needs help to go to the bathroom

    Reduce interactions during potty breaks

    Nighttime potty training

Sneak into parent's bed

    Install a child gate

    Lock parents' door

    Install babyproof device on door knobs

Turns on bedroom lights to prevent sleep

    Install babyproof device on light switch

    Install smart plug on light

    Move furniture so that they can't reach

    Children at this age are prone to knee jerk reactions, they don't always consciously think before acting. Preparing beforehand will allow you to get ahead of these knee jerk actions and leave them with no choice but to call out for you. Here again, your preparation will pay off because you will be able to wake up and correct their behavior instead of falling back on old habits due to exhaustion. Be creative and adjust as you go since you may find that your little one gets creative themselves when they see your new response. When you do find yourself having to reset them in the middle of the night your response should be the same as it was at bedtime. Guide them back to their room or bed and verbal reset them. Check in steadily and verbally reset them as needed until they fall back to sleep. Repeat throughout the night.

As they begin to trust your check ins, you can start lengthening the time between checks to the full five minutes. This way they're more likely to fall asleep and you still get to show them that you will keep your word. It will take time to work your way up, be patient they will get there. Resist the temptation to speed the process along or to take short cuts. Make the most of the learning process by being patient. Let them learn at their own pace. That is how you get long term results, that they will always be able to fall back on.

The early morning hours are often the toughest for children and parents to master. The increased difficulty of these hours, the last two especially, is what makes them so important to long term success. You can make exceptions during the first two to three nights of training and decide to start their days early. Once you start to see them make progress, it's time to start taking those hours more seriously. Use the five-minute rule consistently until the 11th hour. As you get closer to their scheduled wake up, make sure to remind them to wait for their clock to light up or change color. Really emphasize this physical cue so that they learn to focus on it and appreciate its importance. During the 11th hour, your approach should be the same while using the 15-minute patience practice rule instead of the five-minute rule.

When the time comes, be prepared to offer a lot of praise and congratulations, even if they struggled through the night. Tell them how proud you are and can offer them a favorite breakfast as a reward or extra cuddles throughout the day. If they really struggled, reassure them. Let them know how proud you are that they tried and that you'll both try again that night. Keep your day as normal and uneventful as possible.

Prepare for the second night. While children tend to do better, it is not uncommon for the second night to be more difficult than the first. This is especially true if the first night went well. By this age, they will be able to realize that these changes are here to stay. They will come to that realization, over time with your consistent response. Stand firm. Be consistent. You should begin to see noticeable improvement by the third night. Every night after should also show improvement.

Some parents may find that even after sleep training their child takes time to fall asleep or wakes up earlier than they would like. If your child is playing quietly by themselves, it is progress. It's also something that, with time, will improve. Even though they may not be sleeping, they are having less stimulating activity, so they are still getting rest. This behavior is a desirable one since it shows your child's growing independence. Consider it practice and encourage it where/when you can.

Room to Grow

Babycoach case study

Six-year-old Brandon expected his parents to lay with him until he fell asleep. The nighttime routine varied wildly, sometimes lasting two to three hours. Once asleep, he was able to stay asleep for a few hours on his own. Sometime between 2:00 and 4:00 AM he would move to his parents' bed. Nights were unpredictable, uncomfortable, and stressful.

As the weeks passed, Brandon's days started to suffer as well. He began to become increasingly demanding, whiny, unruly, and defiant. Brandon's parents, Tom and Megan, found themselves growing more frustrated, short-fused, resentful, and powerless.

How we trained Brandon

We were initially contacted by Tom and Megan in May. We recommended that training start after Brandon's school year ended. Training started a week after Brandon's last day of school. The week gave him a chance to adjust to his new schedule but not so long that he could grow anxious about training.

A few days before training, we had Tom and Megan start talking to Brandon about teaching him to sleep independently at night. At that point, it was important that he understood that they were not looking for his permission or opinion. This was simply a respectful way to lay out what was planned while establishing Tom and Rachel as being in charge.

Chapter Nine

Next, we focused on setting Brandon up for success. We made some changes to his environment so that it would be more conducive to independent sleep. We introduced a recording of numbers being counted in Spanish as that was his second language and he loved numbers. We wanted the recording to catch his attention with a steady rhythm that would help to slow his thinking process and reactions.

Once his environment was settled, we began to focus on his nighttime routine. Tom and Megan decided on a more streamlined routine they could maintain long-term. The nighttime routine was made a bit more difficult since Brandon was sharing a room with his younger brother, who went to bed 45 minutes earlier. During the routine, we had Megan communicate to Brandon the new limits of the routine. Specifically, she would read him three books and rub his back for two minutes.

Once she finished reading his books, Megan and Brandon moved to his room. There, Megan started a timer and kept to it, while rubbing his back. At the end of the two minutes, she ended the night by saying "good night, I love you. I'll check on you in three minutes".

We all monitored Brandon from outside the room. Luckily for us, Brandon took his role as a big brother seriously and didn't make too much noise. However, he did sit up in his bed while crying. After waiting two minutes, we had Megan "check in" and reset Brandon. It took six rounds of check in/resets before he fell asleep.

During the overnight hours, Brandon woke up twice and called out to his parents. We had them use the same response; check in, verbally reset, and exit. Both times he woke up took two resets.

He woke for good around 6:15 AM. At that point we had Tom go in and remind him to wait for his clock to "wake up". We didn't have Tom tell him to go back to sleep, rather, we had him tell Brandon to wait patiently. He did need a few reminders, but he waited in bed until the clock changed colors.

It took three nights for Brandon to start going to bed without waiting for his parents to check in or any crying. It took much longer, about eight days, for him to stop needing reminders to wait for his clock. The two-week reinforcement period was especially important because of his age.

Chapter Ten

Nap Training

Naps are a necessity. Your baby cannot manage long periods of awake time without consequence. Regular scheduled naps have been shown to improve a baby's mood and overall health, improve cognitive ability, and boost immunity. The sooner parents begin nap training, the sooner your baby will reap these benefits.

Nap training also reinforces the nighttime sleep training. As your baby ages, they will begin to understand that there are different rules in place for naps and nighttime sleep. Parents that do not nap train, often find that their baby begins to regress at night as a result. Sleep train at night first before nap training. The skills your baby learns to help them sleep through the night are the very same skills they will need to develop their naps during the day.

Parents should not expect that the linear progress they saw at night will also occur with naps. Night sleep comes very naturally to us as a species. Daytime naps are a great habit that take time and patience to develop, they are a skill that must be learned.

Three to Six months

Ideally nap training should start between 14-16 weeks. Nap training should occur two weeks after your baby begins to sleep through the night. If, for any reason, your baby is struggling to sleep the final two hours of their nighttime sleep and are older than 14/16 weeks, you should go ahead with nap training.

A great majority of babies naturally want to sleep thirty minutes after ninety minutes of activity time. Parents should aim to lengthen those natural naps by fifteen-minute increments. Once your baby is ready to begin nap training, aim for a minimum of 60 minute in crib practice. This should initially be done 90 minutes to two hours after they've woken up for the day.

Once your baby begins to show signs of being tired, i.e. rubbing their eyes, yawning, etc. you can begin their first nap. Use the same routine, minus the feeding, that you use to put your baby to bed. Use the three-minute rule until your baby falls asleep. This rule should be used for the entire first half of the nap, or 30 minutes.

If your baby falls asleep, allow them to sleep. At this point a nap can last for 90-120 minutes. For the second part of the nap, or after the 30-minute mark, you should use the 15-minute patience practice rule. Ideally you will do two rounds of patience practice. Your baby does not need to be crying intensely to begin the patience practice timer, you should just notice that they are escalating, i.e. they stop happy talking/babbling and start crying. Keep in mind that if your baby wake ups crying that indicates that they are still tired. A rested baby wakes up happy! Use that to motivate yourself to go through patience practice fully.

After two set of 15 minutes patience practice, the nap can be over. Parents should enter their babies' room and start softly talking to them, opening blinds, etc. Ideally your baby will calm slightly before you pick them up. We want to reinforce positive behaviors every chance we can! You should repeat two more times during the day. Babies 12-16 weeks often need at least three one-hour naps after 1.5 to 2 hours of activity time.

Once your baby is older than 16 weeks you should begin to consolidate their naps. Ideally your baby will have a 60-90-minute morning nap, a 120-minute afternoon nap, and a cat nap between the third and fourth feeding. This cat nap should be 30 minutes maximum. Ideally it will occur early enough to ensure your baby has at least 2 hours of activity time before their bedtime.

As your baby gets closer to six months, they will naturally drop that third nap. You may find that there is a transitional period where your baby doesn't need the catnap but can't quite stay awake for the entire four hours. Start the bedtime routine early during this period. It's better to put your baby to bed early than to risk them growing overtired. Maintain their scheduled wake up. If baby goes to bed 30 minutes early, they should NOT be picked up the next day 30 minutes early. The whole point of putting them to bed early is to accommodate their new ability to manage longer periods of time while providing more sleep until they fully adjust. It's easier to maintain them in their crib in the morning after they've had a restful night of sleep, than it is to keep them awake at the end of the day when they're more likely to be overtired than usual.

Chapter Ten

Morning nap Training Schedule

7:00 AM – 7:00 PM Schedule

8:30 – 9:00 AM – Begin morning nap

First 30 minutes, use 3 Minute Rule.

Second 30 minutes, use 15 Minute Rule

9:30 – 10:00 AM – End nap after 60 minutes

Afternoon Nap Training Schedule

7:00 AM – 7:00 PM Schedule

1:00 PM – Begin afternoon nap

First 30 minutes, use 3 Minute Rule

Second 30 minutes, use 15-minute rule

2:00 PM – End nap

Room to Grow

Six to Twelve months

Nap training at this age will depend on your judgement as a parent. While your baby will benefit from nighttime sleep training practice before nap training, parents can nap train at the same time as they are nighttime sleep training. The two-week reinforcement period between nighttime sleep training and nap training isn't as necessary. Nap training at this age will often help the baby to fully master the overnight hours.

At this age your baby will need a 60 to 90-minute nap in the morning and a 120-minute nap in the afternoon. Use the five-minute rule for the first half of the nap and the 15-minute patience practice rule for the second half of the nap. Because we want your baby to sleep for the fully allotted time, take however long it took your baby to fall asleep and whatever time your baby takes to fall back to sleep and add that time to the scheduled end of the nap. This is only something you should do if they are still asleep. This will ensure that your baby is both rested and has an opportunity to practice their skill.

Chapter Ten

Morning nap Training Schedule

7:00 AM – 7:00 PM Schedule

8:30 – 9:00 AM – Begin morning nap

First 30 minutes, use 3 Minute Rule.

Second 30 minutes, use 15 Minute Rule

9:30 – 10:00 AM/ 10:30 AM – End nap after 60/90 minutes

Afternoon Nap Training Schedule

7:00 AM – 7:00 PM Schedule

1:00 PM – Begin afternoon nap

1:00 – 2:00 PM - Use 3 Minute Rule

2:00 – 2:30 PM - Use 15-minute rule

2:30 PM – End nap

Twelve to Eighteen months

At this point your baby will be showing signs of fighting either the morning nap or afternoon nap. As they grow, they can more easily handle longer periods of awake time. We suggest parents develop a single 2-3-hour nap in the middle of the day.

If you have already nap trained your baby, you might start noticing that your baby stays awake through most of the morning nap more often than not, and because of that they can barely make it to their scheduled afternoon nap. That is a clear sign that you should consider eliminating the morning nap and moving the afternoon nap more towards the middle of the day to develop one longer nap in the middle of the day.

Use the five-minute rule for the first half of the nap and the 15-minute rule for the second half of the nap. Be prepared for inconsistent progress when nap training and retraining your baby at this age. This requires greater patience and consistency on the part of the parent to see long term results. Be prepared to put your baby to bed slightly early on days that they do not have a good single nap.

Chapter Ten

Morning nap Training Schedule

7:00 AM – 7:00 PM Schedule

8:30 – 9:00 AM – Begin morning nap

First 30 minutes, use 3 Minute Rule.

Second 30 minutes, use 15 Minute Rule

9:30 – 10:00 AM – End nap after 60 minutes

Afternoon Nap Training Schedule

7:00 AM – 7:00 PM Schedule

1:00 PM – Begin afternoon nap

1:00 – 2:00 PM - Use 3 Minute Rule

2:00 – 2:30 3:00 PM - Use 15-minute rule

2:30 PM – End nap

Eighteen to Thirty-Six months

Nap training at this age is the same as nap training at 12-18 months. Parents should expect their baby to take a single nap of at least 2 hours, in the middle of the day. Keep this nap until 36 months even if they begin to show signs of dropping it. Teaching your toddler to have quiet time will be beneficial in many ways. Not only will your child learn to be patient, the quiet time will be a time of rest.

Afternoon Nap Training Schedule

7:00 AM – 7:00 PM Schedule

1:00 PM – Begin afternoon nap

1:00 – 2:00 PM - Use 3 Minute Rule

2:00 – 3:00 PM - Use 15-minute rule

3:00 PM – End nap

Chapter Eleven

Nightmares/Night Terrors

    Nightmares are normal and common in children under 10. They can occur in children as young as one, but generally start between three and six years of age. Most children will have nightmares occasionally, two to four-year olds are particularly prone. This age is typically when normal fears develop, a child's imagination blossoms, and they can describe a bad dream.

    Nightmares usually have roots or are triggered by events that are occurring in a child's life during the day. We always recommend that parents examine the media that their child is consuming in order to find the most likely cause of their nightmares. Examine books, television shows, movies, and internet content. Media should be age appropriate.

    We also recommend examining their recent emotional environment. Stress can also lead to nightmares and should be kept to a minimum if possible. Major life events may also trigger nightmares. A new school year, family vacation or get together, moving to a new home, etc. can all cause anxiety. Be sensitive to their fear or anxiety about these events and take time to reassure them.

Nightmares can also sometimes happen for no reason at all. If they don't increase in frequency, you shouldn't worry too much. They most likely to occur approximately 90 minutes after your child initially falls asleep. They may wake up from the nightmare and, depending on their age, may be able to remember and describe the bad dream to you. Keep track of when nightmares occur as that can help identify the cause. Take note of your child's dream, as that can also help you pinpoint the cause.

Remain calm throughout a nightmare episode. Children can sense your emotions, staying calm will help them to calm down themselves. If the nightmares persist for a period of time without any improvement, contact your pediatrician for guidance on how to proceed.

While you can't fully prevent nightmares, having a regular sleep routine helps. A dedicated bedtime routine will help them wind down after a long day. When all is quiet, it is a good time to communicate with your child, to bring comfort and reassurance. Getting enough sleep will be a game changer, since stress and exhaustion can increase the likelihood of a nightmare occurring.

Night terrors

Less common than nightmares and can sometimes be referred to as sleep terrors. Usually they occur in children from one to eight years old. They are distinctly different from the far more common

Chapter Eleven

nightmare. They're distinct because children often don't remember them once they wake up.

Night terrors are most likely to occur one to two hours after your child initially goes to sleep. They can occur during nighttime sleep as well as daytime sleep. Children will wake up screaming and the screaming can last up to 30 minutes. During an episode, children can cry, shout, or scream but are not aware of their surroundings or your presence.

Night terrors occur in about two percent of children. Usually, they are not caused by psychological stress, but can be triggered by being overtired. Sometimes, recurring night terrors are a symptom of other sleep disorders like obstructive sleep apnea.

If taking the simple steps, we outline here does not cause improvement, as always, we suggest talking to your pediatrician for a more in-depth analysis.

Symptoms of night terrors can include:

- Partially or fully waking from sleep very suddenly.
- Screaming or thrashing.
- Intense fear or terror from an unknown source.
- Wide eyes with dilated pupils.
- Rapid breathing.
- Racing heart.
- Elevated blood pressure.
- Sweating.

Night terrors usually go away within a week or so. However, if they persist, talk to your doctor. It is common for them to come back several times until your child is older. They are usually completely gone by age 9 of 10.

Help Your Child Keep Night Terrors Away

1. Instill and maintain a routine. Bedtime and wake-up time should remain consistent during the week and weekend.

2. Make sure the area around your child's bed is safe.

3. Keep track of what time the night terrors start and wake up your child about 5/10 minutes before that. Shush and hold them for a few minutes, then walk away. Allow them to go back to sleep. The idea is to interrupt the cycle.

4. Keep a journal of events. It will help your pediatrician immensely if their intervention is necessary.

Chapter Twelve

Nutrition

To truly understand the importance of nutrition in sleep training and your child's overall development, we must first establish what nutrition is. Nutrition is the process of providing or obtaining the food necessary for health and growth. The key words here are health and growth. Health is obvious, every parent's goal is to make sure their baby is as healthy as possible. Growth is slightly less obvious, but just as important when you step back and realize just how much your baby is going to grow and develop within their first five years of life. Making sure that your baby successfully transitions from a perfect food source (breastmilk) to a variety of less perfect foods is a balancing act that every parent must master.

Let's start at the beginning, the first food we always recommend is breastmilk. While there are some truly great formula brands on the market, breastmilk will always be our first choice for newborns and babies. The caveat here is that not all women are created equal in this area. Production will vary, sometimes wildly. The nutrition in breastmilk can depend on the mother's diet. Nature is incredibly forgiving and remarkably resilient. You don't need a perfect diet to produce great quality food for your baby. A good diet certainly helps, but women have been able to feed their babies even in times of famine or extreme hardship. Some women don't particularly like breastfeeding or are unable to do so. If breastfeeding is painful or uncomfortable, pumps and bottles are now available practically everywhere. The key is to find what works best for you and your family.

If breastmilk is not an option, you'll find no judgments from us. We do recommend doing your research and consulting with your pediatrician since there are a lot of factors to consider when choosing a formula. In our experience, most pediatricians recommend formulas made from cow's milk. Nowadays there are organic versions available as well as formulas made from grass-fed cow's milk. If your baby doesn't respond well to traditional formulas, your pediatrician may recommend a soy-based formula or other alternative. If allergies run in your family, especially food-based allergies, there are "hydrolyzed" formulas available and formulas without corn, soy, etc.

Finding the right formula for your baby may take some experimentation, so we do not recommend buying in bulk before your baby arrives. Buy just enough for a week or two, to see how your baby handles that formula specifically. Once you establish that they're digesting it

Chapter Twelve

well and aren't having any adverse reactions, then you can stock up. You may find that you must change formulas later, since your baby's growth may affect how they're able to digest that formula. That's fine and something we see often enough.

When the time comes to introduce solid foods, this is where the balancing act begins. Nowadays, most pediatricians (and in fact the American Academy for Pediatrics) recommend starting solids around six months of age. Before then, babies should be exclusively breast/formula fed. We have seen pediatricians recommend starting solids as early as four months in some cases. There are a few signs you can look for that will indicate that it may be time to start discussing solids with your pediatrician:

- Your infant still seems hungry after getting a full day's allowance of 32 to 36 ounces.
- If nursing, you will notice that your little one seems to want to be longer on the breast than usual or wants to eat more frequently.
- They are more observant especially when you eat. You'll notice them looking attentively, as you guide the food from your plate into your mouth.

Consult their doctor first because they will be able to give you the most accurate information about your baby. They will also typically recommend a food that you should start with. We do suggest that parents aim for an overall balanced diet of vegetables, fruits, proteins, healthy fats, legumes, whole grains, etc. Generally, introducing vegetables first is recommended, since they are the most nutrient dense food category by far. Most babies will end up preferring fruits and carbohydrates (cereals, potatoes, sweet potatoes, etc.) due to the higher sugar content of these foods, so offering vegetables first will give you a greater chance of successfully introducing these foods into your baby's diet.

Right now, you're probably saying "ok but how do we do this?". When first introducing solids or whenever you're offering a new food, offer it at the beginning of the second feeding (lunch). This will give you a greater chance of success, since your baby will be hungry and less likely to be overtired/cranky after their morning nap. At the same time, this will give you the rest of the day to observe and see how they're handling that food. Make note of any digestive issues the food may cause or if they're showing signs of a possible allergy to that food. Once you've given a food to your baby several times, and have established that it's safe, you can begin giving it to them for breakfast and eventually at a more "dinner time" type feeding.

If they do not respond well the first few times you try a new food, because of texture, taste, or simply because it's new, it's not an indication that they don't like that food. They may make funny faces, turn their head away, and sometimes even gag on a food. It may take some time for a baby to adjust. As with all things in the Babycoach method, patience and persistence are key. Offer the same food 4-5 times before trying a different one.

Don't be tempted to offer too many new foods all at once or only offer one food just because that's the only one your baby immediately ate well (often cereal). That's how you get started down the road to a very "picky" eater. Try to establish a balanced diet that meets your baby's needs to maintain optimal health and growth. Before deciding your baby just doesn't like a certain food, try different cooking methods, recipes, new seasonings, etc. Some babies will not learn to like a specific food until they've tried it ten times or more. Just because they may not like a food now, does not mean they won't learn to like it in a month or two. Be patient and keep at it.

Below you'll find a list of great foods to start introducing into your baby's diet and their benefits:

Vegetables

<u>Root</u> <u>Vegetables</u> – Carrot, parsnip, yam, potato, sweet potato, rutabaga, winter squash, butternut squash. These have a natural sweet taste and have a smooth texture when pureed. They are all super foods because of their high nutritional content.

> <u>Carrots</u> - Rich in Beta-carotene (darker older carrots contain more beta- carotene than baby ones)
>
> <u>Butternut</u> <u>squash</u> - easily digested, again lots of beta-carotene
>
> <u>Parsnips</u> – Good source of fiber and starch, antioxidant, Vitamins C and E
>
> <u>Potato</u> – Contain Vitamin C, Potassium, they are glorious and blend well with all other vegetables. Lots of varieties to choose from.

<u>Zucchini</u> –Folate, Potassium, Vitamin C, B-6 and A

<u>Peas</u> – High is Vitamins A, C, and K. Great source of plant protein

<u>Green beans</u> – High in Vitamins K and C, manganese

Fruits

Soft ripe fruit, banana, peach, melon, papaya, avocado can be eaten raw. Tougher, or fibrous, fruits like apple and pear should be cooked until softened.

<u>Prunes/Plums</u> – Vitamin A, C, Fiber

<u>Avocado</u> – Rich in Fiber, healthy fats, Vitamin A, Vitamin K, Vitamin B6, Folate

<u>Banana</u> – Full of carbohydrates that provide sustained energy, potassium, fiber, vitamin C

<u>Papaya</u>– Rich in Vitamin C, Beta Carotene, high in Fiber and has Enzymes that aid digestions

<u>Pears</u> – One of the least allergenic foods. Contain fiber and Vitamin C.

<u>Cantaloupe</u> – Rich in Vitamin C and Beta carotene

<u>Peaches</u> – Easy to digest, soft flesh and an excellent source of Vitamin C and A

<u>Apples</u> – Dietary fiber and Vitamin C.

Cereals

Single grain varieties such as rice, barley, or oats should be cooked until softened. May be served with formula or breastmilk as a mix in.

<u>Rice</u>- Rice was for a long time, the first choice of cereal to be introduced, because it is bland and easy to digest, creating less allergies. Lately there has been some concern and research about the arsenic levels being too high. The best way to cook the rice and to reduce potential arsenic levels is to cook the rice in plenty of water (about six to 10 parts water to one part of rice). Begin by rinsing the rice several times before you start the boiling process, this will help wash away some of the arsenic. Cook until the rice is very tender, usually 20-25 minutes over medium low heat. You will have a creamy liquid that you can then cool off and add to pureed bananas, squashes, papaya, avocado, sweet potatoes, etc. Store it in a glass container in the fridge for use throughout the week.

<u>Oats</u> – Should be prepared using the same method as the rice without the rinsing. Boil oats, regular or steal cut (six cups of water to one cup of oats) until they reach the creamy consistency, you are after, thicker or thinner is a matter of taste. There are ready to feed oat cereal for babies, so that is an option as well.

<u>Barley</u> – This is another grain that is low in arsenic. We do recommend soaking the barley for a couple of hours before cooking. Cook the barley (6 cups of water for 1 of barley) until the grains are very tender. You will have a rich cream, drain and store in the fridge. Mix with veggies and fruits. In this case, there is no warning on harmful content on the ready to feed Barley cereal for babies, so that is an option as well.

Mealtimes, in practice

If you've gotten to our nutritional chapter, chances are you have gone through the sleep training process and seen how positively the process has affected your family's lives. The family dinners so often portrayed in the commercials we see every day, may seem unattainable. A pipe dream of a time long ago, with our busy schedules and cranky kids. It's not, you can absolutely end the everyday battle of dinner time. You can establish a family meal (or two or three) where you can sit and enjoy a meal together. Where you don't have to prepare extra dishes because your child is a "fussy eater". You will see just as much progress as you did with sleep training. It's simply a matter of taking back the reins, your consistent behavior over time, and establishing boundaries.

First and foremost, 80% of your baby's/child's food should be found in the fridge and 20% in the pantry. Too many foods geared to children are full of processed/refined carbohydrates and sugar. Aim to give your child a rainbow of foods. Don't allow yourself to become restricted to a few choice foods. Focusing on the fridge will ensure that fresh vegetables, fruits, cheese, proteins, etc. will make the bulk of your child's diet while still leaving room for easy snacks and treats.

Take the time to read the nutrition labels on the foods you regularly buy. You'd be surprised by what is in foods that are being marketed as healthy. No matter how tempting it is, do not introduce unneeded salt or sugar to your baby's diet. Excess salt may be harmful to

Chapter Twelve

their kidneys and sugar is addictive. Natural sugars are enough for their first year. "Healthy" or "organic" junk food is still just that, junk food. We've all heard the horror stories of kids who will "only" eat mac & cheese or chicken nuggets. Even if that mac & cheese is organic and made with pasture raised, grass fed cheese or the chicken in the nuggets is antibiotic free and organic, they're still not healthy options long term if they're the only foods your child is eating. A little bit of effort now, will give you a lifetime of reassurance that your child's diet is well-rounded.

Meals should occur at a table or counter. Take 30 minutes out of everyone's day, so the entire family can be present. While this may not be possible all the time, this does give the family a chance to connect and have each other's undivided attention. Take the time to set the table, make it an activity your child helps with. Resist the urge to eat in front of a tv or tablet. Encourage them to focus on their meal and eat their food without outside distractions. Turn off electronics entirely if need be. Make dinner a family ritual and your child will learn, just as they did when you established a nighttime routine, what is being expected of them during this time.

Meal Prepping

Nowadays, parents are busier than ever. Between jobs, juggling multiple schedules, schools/daycare, etc. it can be near impossible to find the time, not to mention the energy, to cook a meal at home every night. If you don't have the time to cook every night, that's fine.

Remind yourself that you pay for convenience, one way or another.

When it comes to your baby's food, we do recommend buying fresh foods and cooking at home. This will help you avoid preservatives, unneeded added sugars, overcooked foods (with less nutrients), too much salt, etc. By cooking at home, you will be able to control all these factors and oftentimes end up with a much better result for much less.

Once a week, or once every two weeks, think about what you'd like to serve for breakfast, lunch, and dinner and create a family meal plan. This is an excellent opportunity to be creative, since you can use the same foods in new ways throughout the week. Try to do this on the same day every week or two, since again, consistency is key. This will give you the chance to create a shopping list for the grocery store.

Once you're back from the store, meal prepping can begin. It can be as simple as pre-chopping veggies that you'll use later in the week or as involved as cooking everything at once. Do what works best for you, taking the week ahead in to account. There will be some weeks that are especially busy where you'll do more on the meal prep days and other weeks where you'll do very little. Even if you don't cook everything on this day, having a few things ready i.e. veggies already chopped or diced, a cooked protein, etc., will make it easier for you to throw something together with minimal effort. This will get you ahead and make it easier for you to resist the temptation to grab something that's quick and easy but oftentimes very unhealthy. A little meal prepping goes a very long way!

Chapter Twelve

Meal Prepping by age

Six Months

Start on Monday since that will give you the weekend to cook the grains, if that is where you are starting, or the vegetable of your choice. Just two vegetables should be enough for the first six to ten days. Offer one vegetable, i.e. carrot, only then you can try offering the other vegetable, i.e. sweet potato

Allow three to four days to see how your baby's digestive system reacts to the new foods. This will also give your baby a chance to adjust to the new taste and textures of this new food. You can mix a tablespoon of the vegetable puree with a tablespoon of breast milk or formula to help your baby adjust. Your baby will start small, only eating a tablespoon or two.

Sample First week

Sunday - Cooking day

Steam a few carrots until they are tender. Puree them until they are a smooth consistency, reserving about a half cup for the first three days. Freeze any remaining carrot puree in baby food freezer containers. They will last in the freezer for several months.

Bake a sweet potato in the oven until very soft to the touch. Cut in half while still warm and scoop the sweet potato out of the skin and puree it. Reserve about a ½ cup. Freeze any leftover in baby food freezer containers.

Monday - Wednesday/Thursday

Offer carrot puree, 2 to 3 teaspoons at the start of one meal, before breast or bottle feeding. You can mix a tablespoon of vegetable with a tablespoon of breast milk or formula.

Thursday/Friday – Sunday

Offer sweet potato puree, 2 to 3 teaspoons at the start of one meal (lunch). Again, you can mix a tablespoon with a tablespoon of breast milk or formula to help them adjust.

Sample Second week

Sunday - Cooking day

Bake two or three seeded zucchinis in the oven until soft to the touch. While still warm, scoop the zucchini out of the skin so that you can puree it. Reserve about a ½ cup. Freeze any leftover in baby food freezer containers.

Bake winter squash until it can be pierced with a knife. Scoop out, while still warm, and puree. Reserve

Chapter Twelve

about a ½ cup and freeze the remaining winter squash in baby food freezer containers.

Monday - Wednesday/Thursday

Offer zucchini puree, two to three teaspoons at the start of one meal, before your baby breast or bottle feeds. You can mix a tablespoon of vegetable with a tablespoon of breast milk or formula to help them adjust.

Thursday/Friday – Sunday

Offer winter squash puree, two to three teaspoons at the start of one meal. Again, you can mix a tablespoon vegetable with a tablespoon of breast milk or formula to help them adjust.

Sample Third week

Sunday - Cooking day

Grind whole or old-fashioned oats in a food processor until they reach a finely ground powder consistency. Boil oats in water until very tender, about eight to ten minutes. A good ratio is a quarter cup of finely ground oats for every cup of water. Oatmeal should be very creamy. May be served with mashed bananas, apple, avocados, or vegetables you baby has already tried

Boil a couple of apples with a couple of tablespoons of water until very soft. You may also try baking apples. Puree the apples until very smooth. Reserve 1/2 cup and freeze any leftovers in baby food freezer containers.

Monday – Wednesday/Thursday

Offer two to three teaspoons of oatmeal at the start of a meal. If the oatmeal has set and is too firm, you may add a tablespoon of breast milk or formula to help it reach a creamier consistency.

Thursday/Friday - Sunday

Offer two to three teaspoons (or more if your baby seems interested) of apple sauce at the start of the meal. You can mix a tablespoon with a tablespoon of breast milk or formula if needed.

Sample Fourth week

Sunday - Cooking day

Rinse several cups of organic brown rice until the water used runs clear. Soak in cold fresh water for six hours, this will help to make it easier to digest. Rinse slightly and drain fully. Spread the rice on a paper towel lined baking sheet and allow to dry completely. Once dry, the rice can be processed in a food processor until it becomes a fine powder. This powder can be saved in the refrigerator in a glass container for several weeks. To cook, use a 1:6 ratio of rice powder to water. Combine 1 tablespoon of rice powder to half a cup of water in a heavy bottom saucepan. Bring to a boil and cook until it reaches a very creamy consistency.

Buy two to three ripe bananas. Aim for them to be overripe when you serve them. This will better help your baby digest their starches.

Monday – Wednesday/Thursday

Offer four to five tablespoons (or more if your baby seems interested) rice cereal porridge at the start of one meal. You can mix the three to four tablespoons of rice cream porridge with a tablespoon of breast milk or formula

Thursday/Friday

Mash 1/3 of a banana until very creamy. You can mix the mashed banana with 2 to 3 tablespoons of rice cereal porridge or 1 tablespoon of breast milk or formula. Offer at the start of one meal.

Seven Months

Introduce Breakfast. Second solid feeding

You should now be able to stop adding a tablespoon of breastmilk or formula to your baby's solid foods. They should have had enough time to adjust to the new flavors and textures making this step unnecessary. You can also begin offering solids at two feedings, ideally breakfast and lunch. This will give you an opportunity to observe your baby before bed, so that you can spot any digestive issues that may occur due to new foods.

You can begin introducing meat at this time. Pasture raised, organic sources of meat are preferable since they will offer the most nutrition and help your baby get more iron, zinc, and protein in their diet. Try introducing beef, chicken, turkey and low-mercury fish such as sole, haddock, or trout.

Herbs, oils, and spices can now be used to flavor foods. Basil, thyme, parsley, turmeric, ginger, coriander, dill, etc. are all great options. Finally, you may also begin introducing nut butters at this time. Speak to your pediatrician before doing so. The latest research has begun to suggest that introducing nut butter early can decrease the likelihood of allergy later.

Chapter Twelve

Sample First Week

Sunday - Cooking Day

Boil potatoes until very soft. Puree or mash them until very smooth. You can add some extra virgin cold pressed olive oil to flavor them.

Defrost the carrots and apples you previously cooked. Simply place the freezable container in the refrigerator, it takes about 24 hours to fully thaw.

Boil chicken until very soft. May be served with fresh herbs such as dill or rosemary, and a drizzle of cold pressed extra virgin olive oil. Chop or shred chicken until it is very fine. Add to either the carrots or potatoes.

Soften a couple of pears by boiling them with a few tablespoons of water and a cinnamon stick. Once tender, puree the pears. You may add extra cinnamon when serving.

Monday – Wednesday/Thursday

<u>Breakfast</u>

Offer two to three tablespoons of pureed pear. Your baby can always have more if you believe they want it.

<u>Lunch</u>

Offer new vegetable, and two to three tablespoons of potato puree mixed with chicken.

Thursday/Friday – Sunday

Breakfast

Two to three tablespoons (or more) of apple sauce. Can be served with cinnamon or pumpkin pie spice.

Lunch

Carrot puree mixed with chicken. At this point your baby will be eating around 4 to 6 ounces of solids. Once you introduce a protein, this may reduce slightly. They may also eat slightly less at this feeding, since the chicken requires more chewing.

Sample Second week

You can begin cooking foods together to create baby food "mashes". By this point your baby should be able to eat more textured foods that require more chewing.

Sunday - Cooking Day

Boil meat (beef, turkey, or chicken, it's your choice) and vegetable (potatoes, carrots, leeks, scallion etc.) much like you would a stew. The combination is up to you. We recommend using foods you already know your baby can digest well and incorporating one new food (i.e. if the protein you use is new, use known vegetables.) Cook until very tender and mash it until smooth with a few smaller chunks remaining. Reserve enough for three to four days and freeze the rest.

Cook some rice cereal porridge. Use a one to six ratio. Store it in a glass container in the fridge to be used during the week

Frozen vegetables/fruits– It's time to defrost and use your frozen veggies and fruits since your baby will begin eating foods with more texture. This is an ideal time to use the smoother consistency foods you previously saved.

Monday – Wednesday/Thursday

Breakfast

Two to three tablespoons of rice cereal porridge. May be served with mashed banana or avocado for added texture. Cinnamon can also be used to introduce new seasonings.

Lunch

A few tablespoons of sweet potato puree mixed with some of the meat mash.

Thursday/Friday – Sunday

Breakfast

Two to three tablespoons of pureed pear. May be served with another mashed fruit such as banana, avocado, or berries.

Lunch

Three to four tablespoons of meat mash and some left over veggies.

Sample Third Week

Sunday – Cooking day

Bake or boil meat with veggies. Try to leave things a bit more textured every week or so when mashing.

Prepare Barley cereal porridge to a slightly less creamy consistency.

Defrost zucchini and winter squash.

Monday – Friday

Breakfast

Mashed bananas served with yogurt. Try to choose a yogurt that is lower in sugars and opt for plain yogurt if possible. Greek yogurt or Icelandic Skyr are great options.

Lunch

Meat/Veggie mash. May offer mashed fruit after as a dessert. Try softer fruits that can be mashed without cooking such as bananas, peaches, berries, etc.

Chapter Twelve

Sample Fourth week

Sunday - Cooking day

Boil some chicken until tender the add kale or spinach. Cook for a few more minutes and mash. May be added to a previously frozen vegetable puree if it is too chunky.

Cut a butternut squash in half and bake until it can be easily pierced by a knife. While still warm, scoop out and mash until its slightly creamy with small chunks remaining.

Grind whole or old-fashioned oats in a food processor until they reach a finely ground powder consistency. Boil oats in water until very tender, about eight to ten minutes. A good ratio is a quarter cup of finely ground oats for every cup of water. Oatmeal should be very creamy. May be served with mashed bananas, apple, avocados, or vegetables you baby has already tried

Monday – Wednesday/Thursday

<u>Breakfast</u>

Oatmeal with soft, mashed fruit.

<u>Lunch</u>

Chicken with mixed vegetables\

Thursday/Friday – Sunday

Breakfast

Yogurt with fresh fruit

Lunch

Butternut squash with a bit of chicken

Eight to Nine Months

Your baby should be ready to have two solid meals per day of mashed, not pureed food. You can begin expanding your options by adding more complex carbohydrates and legumes. Whole wheat pasta, brown rice, quinoa, beans, and lentils would all be excellent additions to your baby's diet.

You can also begin to add more vegetables that require chewing such as broccoli, cauliflower, bell peppers, etc. that all do well with less cooking. You may also add natural sweets such as dates or raisins, but we recommend feeding these in moderation.

They should now be able to eat most of the foods that you eat, so it's time to start eating as a family. This is a great time to start establishing a dinner time feeding. The only change we'd recommend you make when preparing family meals is to season (salt/pepper) foods at the table since most babies prefer blander foods.

Chapter Twelve

Sample Meal Plan

Sunday - Cooking day

This month, focus on transitioning your baby to the foods the rest of the family is eating. Whatever you are cooking for the week, just add a little extra for baby.

Precook vegetables you intend to eat throughout the week. Baking and steaming vegetables help preserve nutrients and prevent overcooking which can happen when boiling.

Cook a complex carbohydrate. Pasta is a great choice since it's so versatile and can easily be mixed with vegetables or proteins. We recommend smaller pasta shapes that can be easily chewed and swallowed.

Cook one or two proteins. Bake with olive oil and herbs. Use minimal salt, we recommend none, and no pepper.

Get ahead of the week rush by getting some of the ingredients washed, cut, and ready to go.

Monday – Wednesday/Thursday

<u>Breakfast</u>

Mashed soft fruits with yogurt.

<u>Lunch</u>

Vegetables with a little bit of protein (2/3 vegetable to 1/3 protein).

Dinner

> Whatever the family is having.

Thursday/Friday – Sunday

Breakfast

> Oatmeal with nut butter

Lunch

> Pasta with sauce. Mashed vegetables

Dinner

> Whatever the family is having

Nine months to Twelve months

Sample Meal Plan

Sunday

> Cooking day. Whatever you go for, whether it's a casserole, shepherd's pie, chicken pot pie, cook it today. Whatever you choose can be dinner for a couple of nights, keep that in mind when choosing what to prepare and when. For instance, you can roast a chicken on Monday and use the leftovers in chicken pot pie on Tuesday.

Chapter Twelve

Monday

Shared food - Roasted chicken with potatoes, red/green peppers, onions, parsnips

<u>Baby</u> <u>modification</u>

Mash the veggies all together for your baby, add some frozen vegetables from last months to create a slightly creamier consistency.

<u>Parent</u> <u>modification</u>

Add a salad or a grain to serve with.

Tuesday

Shared food - left over roasted chicken with butternut squash ravioli. Serve with basil, garlic, green onions, (all finely chopped) and cold pressed extra virgin olive oil. Fruit for dessert.

<u>Baby</u> <u>modification</u>

Left over mashed vegetables, finely chopped roasted chicken and butternut squash ravioli (cook a few more minutes than parents ravioli) with basil and olive oil.

<u>Parent</u> <u>modification</u>

Serve with parmesan cheese and a green salad or garlic bread

Wednesday

Shared food - slow cooker stew

Use your favorite recipe. Consider adding extra vegetables for the baby (and yourself!).

<u>Baby modification</u>

Mash the stew, leaving a few small chunks. The idea is to expose your babies to bigger pieces, while being aware of pieces being too big and becoming a choking hazard. You can add a precooked grain such as quinoa or pasta.

<u>Parent modification</u>

Slow cooked stew and a salad or crusty bread.

Thursday

Shared food - Sautéed flounder, baked sweet potatoes with cranberries, and roasted broccoli

<u>Baby modification</u>

Can eat all of it simply make sure its appropriate size.

<u>Parent modification</u>

Just add a salad and seasonings.

Chapter Twelve

Friday

Shared food - Red Beans and Rice. Choose any recipe you like, simply omit things like hot sauce, spices, etc. Save those for the table. Be generous with vegetables and herbs like cilantro.

<u>Baby modification</u>

Can eat as is. Consider adding any vegetables you have precooked in the fridge

<u>Parent modification</u>

Season to your taste.

Saturday

Shared food - buttered pasta with sautéed corn, peas, asparagus. Yogurt with mandarin wedges or raspberries for dessert.

<u>Baby modification</u>

Choose a smaller pasta shape, otherwise they can eat everything as is.

<u>Parents</u>

Add a side salad or bread. Serve with parmesan cheese.

Room to Grow

12 months and beyond

By now your baby should be having three solid meals, breakfast, lunch, and dinner, and a bottle/nursing in the middle of the afternoon. You may begin offering solids during the third "snack" feeding if you're using a four-hour schedule.

By this point, most babies are showing signs that they want to feed themselves. Keep that in mind when deciding what foods to make during the week, because things are going to get messier! While you should encourage them to feed themselves, take time to encourage utensil use as well. It will take time to develop the necessary eye hand coordination, practice will help. Choose foods that they can easily feed themselves by hand. Peas, blueberries, pomegranates, blackberries, and cheese are great options. Utensil use can be saved for warmer foods, which aren't as finger friendly.

The meal plans you use should be the same as the nine to twelve-month sample meal plan. Your baby should be eating what you are with only slight modifications. You should be able to get away with even fewer modifications. They should be able to larger sized pastas, foods shouldn't need to be mashed or pureed, etc. Meal prepping at this point should be all about the family. The only modification that should really remain is seasoning. We still recommend parents wait to salt and pepper foods since most babies don't care for pepper and excess sodium isn't good for them. Other than that, the sky and your imagination is the limit.

Chapter Twelve

Establishing Good Meal Habits in older children

It's so easy to establish bad habits. Often, they're the result of great intentions. You want your baby to be happy. You want the crying to stop. You want to make sure your baby eats something. We've all been there. Bad habits happen, no sense in beating yourself up. Once you realize that these habits aren't working for you or your child, you can begin to change for the better. To start, you need to realize that you are in charge. That is indisputable. Your child can throw a tantrum. They can scream their little hearts out, but at the end of the day only you can go buy that junk food they're demanding. Only you can make that mac & cheese or bake those nuggets. As out of control as the situation may feel, as you may feel, you are in control. You have the power.

Start your child's diet reset with a pantry clean up. Donate any unhealthy foods to your local food bank. There is always someone in need of a treat. Anything that can't be donated should be tossed. Focus on the unhealthy items first or the foods that your child is overly fixated on, you know the ones. They will dig in their little heels and put up a fight. That's okay. Remember, you're in control.

You can easily find healthy alternatives to old favorites if you just take a little time to do so. Keep in mind, you're not trying to substitute one bad habit for a new bad habit, "organic" junk food is still junk food. Make the most of this step to really eliminate these unhealthy foods. Healthy substitutions should be reserved for changes like switching from regular pasta to organic whole wheat pasta or from white to brown rice. Switching your old mac & cheese to an "organic" mac & cheese defeats the purpose of this step if your child is still only going to be eating mac & cheese. Be honest and be thorough.

    Once your pantry has been cleaned up, it's time to go to the grocery store. While you can certainly take your child with you to get their input, know that this may make it tougher to not buy old favorites. Focus on the perimeter of the store, this is where you'll find fresh fruits and vegetables, meats, cheeses, yogurts, etc. Remember, 80% of their diet should be found in your refrigerator. Stock up on healthy foods. Avoid junk foods. Treats can be reintroduced later once you've taught your child to eat a healthier, well balanced diet.

    Once home from the grocery store, take time to meal prep. Wash your fruits and vegetables so that they're ready to eat. Prepare a meal or two. Be ready for a tantrum that is sure to come with the next meal.

    Once you're ready to begin resetting your child's diet, you must be willing to see it through. Make peace with the reality that your "picky" eater might refuse to eat dinner in protest of the new rules. Understand that only hunger can trigger the desire to eat new or different foods. Don't be afraid of your child going to bed hungry. Offer a healthy snack, a piece of fruit or vegetable. If your child again refuses to eat, accept it. Children can very quickly learn that they can skip eating a healthy dinner and still receive a candy bar masquerading as a healthy bar. If they're only hungry for junk, then they're not yet hungry. Put them to bed as per usual and be ready in the morning with a healthy breakfast. You'll see that very quickly they will start eating the occasional healthy meal. It may not be completely consistent yet, with them eating at every meal, but you will see that they begin to eat more often than not. The biggest challenge here will be you and not them. They'll protest and throw tantrums sure, but it's so easy to be consumed by the fear that our child is going to be hungry as a parent. As much as your child is being taught a new way to eat, you are also being taught a new way to feed them. One that requires more work and more thought. One that is nowhere near as easy. Accepting and embracing your power, and your role in this situation, will be your greatest challenge. Be consistent. Keep mealtimes regular and try to avoid giving frequent snacks. Remember, hunger is what will trigger their desire to eat complete healthy meals. You will see positive results.

After a period, you can always introduce the occasional treat back into your child's diet. They're kids after all, what's life without the occasional cupcake or chocolate? Treats are an event or item (i.e. food) that is out of the ordinary. The key here is moderation. If most of your child's diet is healthy and their "ordinary" is focused on healthy eating, treats can be reintroduced without a problem. Be mindful with these treats, because your child has had previous bad habits relating to foods, it's very easy to slide into old bad habits or to develop new ones.

Chapter Thirteen

Discipline

Discipline is a touchy subject in the world of parenting. In and of itself, discipline is the training that corrects, molds, or perfects the mental faculties or moral character (Merriam Webster dictionary definition). Discipline is the teaching or developing of self-control and positive behaviors. It's at the heart of parenting.

Over the years, there have been so many parenting styles that have been *the* way to parent. There are those that have advocated for a more hands-off approach, letting kids figure things out on their own at their own pace. Attachment style parenting brought us the "helicopter" parent. On the complete opposite side of the spectrum, there are those that advocated for corporal punishment and a more domineering approach. Any style of parenting you can think of, has its own loyal following of supporters. What's a parent to do? Let your child take the lead? Protect them from absolutely everything at all times? Bully them into submission? The answer requires us to go back to the heart of parenting. Discipline. It's just that simple and that difficult. It's taking the time to teach your child boundaries, what is expected of them. It's teaching them how to behave in a variety of situations. It's upholding those boundaries consistently, even when they make it difficult. It's parenting 101.

To begin this process, take a moment to close your eyes and imagine the person you would like your child to grow to be. Really think about it. Do you want them to be kind? Curious? Polite? Whoever you want them to be starts right now. Every parent feels like it was only yesterday that they were bringing this brand-new little person home. The weeks felt like seconds, the months like minutes, and the years feel like they happen in a blink. By taking the time to sit and actively think long term, you will be able to give yourself a goal to strive for, a tentative roadmap to follow. Chances are your child won't just wake up at five and say "I'm going to start saying please and thank you from now on". While you may get lucky, most positive traits are actually behaviors developed over time.

Take the time to really think about which behaviors you want to cultivate and then brainstorm ways to make them happen. If you want your child to be polite, be prepared to remind them a million times "what do we say when someone does something nice?" or "how do we ask nicely?". If you want them to be curious, be prepared to answer every question no matter how repetitive or asinine. Get in the habit of asking questions yourself and make seeking out information an adventure. The point, is to know how you want to respond beforehand so that you are prepared for those tough times. Most importantly, be those things you want your child to be. Be polite, curious, calm, they are after all observing and learning from you at all times.

Discipline starts with you

To teach your child discipline, you must first develop it in yourself. It starts with you accepting your role. You are in charge. You are the captain of this team, the general leading these troops. Accept it. Embrace it. Being in charge comes with certain awesome responsibilities but it comes with several perks as well.

The next step of developing personal self-discipline, is accepting that you are human too. You have your strengths and you have your weaknesses. There is only so much stress you can manage at a time before losing it. To develop discipline, you have to learn to put yourself first sometimes. We know! This goes against so much parenting doctrine, but it's true. Sometimes, to be the best parent you can possibly be, you have to put yourself first.

When you first become a parent, you come to the realization that life is going to be a lot less about you and a whole lot more about your baby. It's a realization we all have and its ok. You are expanding yourself and your family. They need to be priority over all for a bit. As time passes, that need lessens and you can begin to start prioritizing yourself too on occasion. Your new role as a parent is a long term one. Go ahead take that yoga class. Go on a date! Grab coffee with a friend. Without a doubt, when you're back with your little one you'll be a better parent for it.

Take the time to meet your own physical needs; sleep through the night, eat meals regularly, take a shower with the door closed. Little things, that make all the difference. Taking care of your own needs will give you the mental and emotional fortitude to weather all of your child's highs and lows.

The same self-care principle applies in the moment. Children have the spectacular, unerring ability to leave even the most put together person off their game. Everything goes out the window the second a tantrum starts. The next time your child throws a tantrum take a second to focus on yourself. Is it difficult for you to think clearly? Is your breathing escalated? Taking the time to really focus on how you and your body responds to the stress of your child's tantrum will give you the chance to learn to center yourself before addressing the tantrum. If you could barely string together a coherent thought, get in the habit of counting to 10. If your breathing was shallow and far too rapid, practice controlled-breathing. Find a solution that will help you pause to gather yourself. Practice these techniques regularly and they will become second nature. Remember parenting is a marathon, not a sprint, practice accordingly.

Resetting your child

Before we really delve into how to teach your child there are two points that need to be addressed. The first is that a child's emotional health, i.e. their ability to process and manage their own emotions, is directly correlated with good sleep habits, healthier eating, and an overall better physical wellbeing. Long-term studies are beginning to show this more and more. Second, while we will give you a few simple steps to help guide you, the secret to long term success is for you to ultimately tailor these steps to fit you. Your personality, history, and lifestyle are unique. While you may find short term success, it's difficult to maintain things long term if that is not taken in to account. For instance, if you are very laid back, a very hands-on approach (i.e. helicopter parenting) may work for a while but chances are your personality won't be able or willing to maintain that approach for years on end. Take these steps as guidelines, rather than hard and fast rules. Adjust them to fit you and you will find long term success.

Room to Grow

Tantrum Step One

"Pausing helps you refrain from making a permanent decision based on a temporary emotion."

Justin Bariso.

Pause. Take a moment to gather yourself. When we're overwhelmed by emotions or stressful situations, the best version of ourselves is not the one that usually shows up. Sometimes to our own surprise we may find ourselves raising our voices, saying hurtful things or bursting into tears. If you're raging with resentment or crushed by disappointment, you're probably not capable of the reasoning required to see a situation in a new light. Pausing will give you the chance to bring down your emotions to a place where you can manage yourself and consciously decide how you'd like to respond.

It helps to take a few deep breaths, step away from the volatile situation or what is triggering the emotional turmoil so you can collect yourself. We've all heard the airplane in distress advice, you must put the oxygen mask on yourself first before you can help your baby or child. The same applies here, you cannot help anyone if you too, are emotionally drowning. Pause, gather yourself.

Chapter Thirteen

Tantrum Step Two

Distract. It takes several years before a child is able to fully process and manage their emotions. They literally can't help but to have the occasional meltdown. Once you've gotten a hold of yourself and can approach them from a better place your primary goal should be distraction.

Distracting them will give them a chance to ride the emotional wave until it dissipates. Your response should be dictated by your child's actions and their personality. If your child is likely to lash out, use physical reassurance such as a firm hug. This will give them the emotional reassurance they need, while also keeping them from injuring themselves or others. If your child likes games, use that to distract them. "I spy" is a great example. Make them focus on something specific in their environment. Shapes, colors, and patterns are all great things that will likely catch their attention. Language is also a great distraction tool. Reciting the alphabet or counting can work well, as can singing favorite songs. As they get older, physical activities can also become an option, i.e. taking a walk. A few minutes of fresh air does wonders for one's mood and will give you a chance to further calm yourself.

The caveat here is that we're not trying to reward any negative behaviors. If your child is having a tantrum about something specific your response should never be to give them what they're demanding. Giving a positive reward to a negative behavior, even one they can't quite control yet, is a surefire way to ensure more explosive tantrums in the future.

Room to Grow

Tantrum Step Three

Correct the behavior. Once the initial emotional wave has passed, this is your opportunity to teach your child. This is best done right after or shortly after they have exhibited the behavior. Teach them privately, away from siblings or other family members. Neither of you needs the added scrutiny and all of the emotions that come with it.

Present the correction in way that shows that your goal is to help them. If they refused to listen and threw a tantrum over a toy ask them "would it help you be a better listener if I took this toy away until a little bit later?" Allow them an opportunity to try again. If they continue to the negative behavior then take the toy after three attempts and they can try again tomorrow. Children will try, but at times their natural impulses will get the best of them. If they threw a tantrum over leaving the park you can ask them "would it help you leave the park if we used a timer". Use the timer to give them a few more minutes of playtime. Once the timer is done remind them of the compromise. If they still continue their tantrum (or start it up again) simply say "we will try coming to the park again when you are calmer".

There will come a time where the behavior will require a more formal form of discipline, a direct reaction to their behavior. These consequences should be used sparingly and saved for these rare occurrences since they can lose their effectiveness if used too often. Always remind yourself that these consequences are just another opportunity for you to teach your child,

Chapter Thirteen

they're not an excuse to mete out harsh punishments. Make sure you can follow through with the disciplinary action you decided to go with, because a consistent behavior is what is going to bring long term results.

Once the issue is resolved, don't hold a grudge. Don't keep bringing up the behavior to family or friends, especially not in front of your child. It's ok to share our experiences with the ones we love, but do it in private. Little ears have a way of hearing things that you may not want them to and they may not understand your intentions. Be mindful of their feelings. Shame is never an emotion that leaves a positive impact.

Chapter 14

Frequently Asked Questions

Can I sleep train while breastfeeding?

Absolutely! The human body is a magnificent piece of machinery, it will produce on demand. Around 8 weeks your baby will start to show signs of losing interest during the night feedings. Babies will naturally show this if you use nursing solely to feed your baby and not as a soothing tool. Your baby needs time to digest, just as your body needs time to produce.

If you're nursing more frequently than every 3 hours, we suggest you establish a three-hour schedule. By slowly moving feedings by 10 minutes this can be achieved with relative ease.

Our aim is to make your baby a little bit hungrier so that when the feeding does occur, they feed a little more vigorously. This will ultimately help to signal to your body that your baby is ready for more food, thereby triggering greater production. This will make stretching the feedings that much easier.

Once you've established a consistent three-hour schedule, for at least 3 days, and you feel that your baby is satisfied, you can begin moving towards a four-hour schedule. Use the same technique and you should find the same success. This process should be very natural.

Our experience has shown that around 10 weeks your baby will begin to naturally drop nighttime feeds. Eliminating nighttime nursing should not diminish your supply, it will just increase the production during the day, while giving your body some relief and the opportunity to recover during the night. You may want to consider incorporating pumping into your own nighttime routine. It may help to reassure you, giving you peace of mind about your overall production. It will certainly help you sleep more comfortably, for a longer period of time.

These suggestions also apply for mothers solely breastfeeding multiples. It will take more time and patience, but it can certainly be done. As always parents should consult their pediatrician since individual health and production does vary.

Chapter Fourteen

When should I pump if I am trying make sure my baby is getting the amount they need and want to increase my production?

It depends on your baby. If they are good at latching, during the day, you can pump a few minutes before nursing. This will enhance the chances of your baby draining your supply which will allow them to reach that fat milk that can only be reached if the breasts are emptied. You can also pump after your baby has finished nursing for at least 5 minutes. Whatever works best for you and your baby. Just keep in mind pumps are not as efficient as a hungry baby. At night, pump just before you go to bed. This will increase the amount of time you can rest before discomfort sets in.

What if I don't like nursing?

There are some hard truths that most don't want to acknowledge, that we feel must be addressed.

Breastfeeding is a personal choice, that should be done in the privacy of your home with your partner.

- Not all breastmilk is the same.

- Breastmilk production varies wildly. While you can do things to increase production, this is only so effective with some women.

- Not all women like breastfeeding, that's ok.

- Not all babies latch

Ultimately, this is a personal decision. Make the best one for you and your family. If you are ready with a great quality formula, you baby should continue to grow and thrive.

When and how do I stop swaddling my baby?

We find that babies often experience increased discomfort between weeks 6 and 8. Once they've stabilized, you should begin to eliminate the swaddle. Ideally this will occur between weeks 8 and 10. There are two ways to eliminate the swaddle.

The first is a more gradual approach. Begin by swaddling under one or both arms. Once the baby has adjusted, you can then begin to swaddle under both arms. Finally, you can begin to loosen the swaddle to give their legs greater freedom. Most babies adjust to each phase within 3-4 nights.

The second approach is to eliminate it entirely all at once. Your baby will have a tougher time adjusting the first few nights, so be prepared to offer plenty of assistance. However, you will see results much faster using this approach.

Whichever approach you choose, be proactive during the day. Plenty of back and tummy time will make the elimination process more efficient. The more time your baby spends practicing the easier their adjustment will be. Don't be tempted to take a short cut with suits that promise to help your baby sleep. They will inhibit your baby's learning and will cause eventual sleep regressions despite sleep training.

Chapter Fourteen

My baby was sleeping through the night by 12 weeks, but now at 17 weeks wakes up occasionally in the middle of the night?

Your baby will go through many phases of development intellectually, physically, and emotionally during their first 24 months. If there is crying after a period of good sleep, don't be afraid to check in on them.

Once you establish that all is well use the 3- or 5-minute rule, until they manage to go back to sleep. The next day observe your baby's demeanor. If there is a cause to the middle of the night wake up, you will be able to catch it during the day. Give your baby three days in a observe pattern. If your baby is coming down with an illness, it will be enough time to see other symptoms. The same is true for teething and other ailments. If it is a physical or emotion development, it is time enough for your baby to adjust.

If after three days, your baby's nights have not gone back to normal begin to reinstate the four basic steps of sleep training. As long as your response to their crying remains consistent, they will always revert back to what they know. True regressions will only occur when you change your response.

My baby just started rolling, can I turn them over in the middle of the night?

If your baby just started and it happened for the first time at night, yes you can. Once your baby figures out how to roll, that's it, you can't stop development.

Be proactive during the day. Plenty of back and tummy time will give your baby more time to practice this new skill. This will also help your baby to become more comfortable in the new position. We recommend 5-10 minutes of practice at least three times a day. Once your baby can roll comfortably, you'll notice that moving them at night becomes futile. At that point stop rolling them.

My baby has been sleeping through the night, but last night they woke up, so I fed them, is that ok?

Once you baby is sleeping through the night you should no longer feed them in the middle of the night. The only exception to this rule is illness. Feeding should never be used to help soothe your baby in the middle of the night. Remember that whatever food your baby consumes in the middle of the night they will not be motivated to eat during next day, which will make them hungry again the next night. Your baby does not care if a feeding comes at 2:00 AM or 2:00 PM, you do so be consistent.

My baby can't stay awake for the entire four hours between the third and fourth feeding, what should I do?

This is completely normal. Babies between three and six months often need a third "catnap" during this time. Make sure this nap lasts no longer than 30 minutes. As your baby gets closer to six months, they will naturally drop this nap.

Chapter Fourteen

We do recommend that this catnap happens at least two hours before their bedtime. That will give your baby enough activity time once they wake up for them to still be tired enough to fall asleep at their scheduled bedtime.

Are solids important or can I delay them? We tried it but my baby really didn't like it!

Solids are very important. You should not delay introducing them. If your pediatrician is recommending it, you should begin to introduce them to your baby's diet. Starting solids is more than just nutrition. A baby learning to eat from a spoon will help to develop their jaw, cheek, and tongue muscle which is necessary for normal speech development.

Giving up, or delaying is not an option. Babies tend to not like change, you will have the feeling that they're fighting you every step of the way. Make peace with it. Your baby will eat well blended foods but rejects chunky food that requires chewing, then chunky foods is what should be offered.

We at Babycoach say that what a baby likes most they get last. Your baby is more likely to eat when they're hungry, so the bottle and favorite foods should come last.

My baby doesn't really need the third nap, but they're delirious at bedtime. What should I do?

As you approach six months you will notice that your baby is able to handle longer periods of awake time but not quite able to handle full four hours before bedtime. During this transitional phase, you can begin your nighttime routine earlier than usual. It is better to put your baby to bed slightly early than for them to become overtired which may make their bedtime much more difficult overall.

Maintain their wake-up time regardless of their actual bedtime, i.e. if you put them down at 6:30 PM you would still pick them up at 7:00 AM. The reason for an early bedtime is the developmental stage, not a change on schedule. This will ensure that their daytime schedule is maintained and that they do end up getting the sleep they need.

Is it ok for my baby to move around all night?

Yes! This is especially true for babies younger than six months. Their brains are still adjusting to consistent sleep cycles. Their bodies are still adjusting to the startle reflex.

Try to not intervene unless your baby cries for longer than three minutes, or your baby gets themselves stuck or in a position they can't get out of. You always want to give your baby the opportunity to try on their own and only step in when the hurdle is too big for them to overcome alone.

Chapter Fourteen

Is it ok to sleep train if my baby wears a helmet?

Absolutely. Helmets are very comfortable. They can retain heat, so parents should keep that in mind when choosing what their baby will wear to bed. The helmet may make movement more difficult, be patient.

As always, be proactive during the day. Give your baby plenty of back and tummy time while using the helmet so that they may practice. We've found that babies adjust to the helmet very quickly and easily.

Can I nap train my baby if they're in daycare during the week?

Usually daycare workers will work with you to maintain your baby's schedule if one exists. However, this will really depend on your daycare and its capabilities. Have open communication, be your baby's advocate.

Try to nap train under similar circumstances. This will increase the chance of success. If your baby is going to be napping in an open room with plenty of outside stimulation, you will want to take that in consideration when training. The daycare may have a set routine that doesn't exactly fit your baby's routine. Depending on how many days you are using the day care services, adjust baby's schedule accordingly. If they spend most days at home use your routine, if most days are spent at daycare, follow their routine.

How do we handle time change and daylight savings time?

Regarding daylight savings time. In the spring, wake the baby 30 minutes earlier and put them to bed 30 minutes early the day before daylight savings begins. You may find that your baby may need another day of early waking/bedtime to adjust. Most babies adjust rapidly and show no signs of change.

In the fall, wake them 30 minutes later. The night before daylight savings time is set to begin, try to put your baby to bed 30 minutes later. You baby should be able to manage 30 minutes of added sleep or awake time with ease. Within 1-2 days your baby should be back to their preferred schedule.

Regarding time zone changes. If you're going on vacation, try to have your baby adjust the way you would. Try to travel in the morning and treat the day as normally as possible. Travel will make your baby more tired than usual, so longer naps may be needed. Babies can have two-hour naps but should also have at least two hours of activity time between naps. Parents should try to get as close to their normal bedtime as possible.

If you find that your baby struggles to stay asleep, don't try to compensate with extra feedings or additional help. We know what is causing the disruption, be patient. Your baby should be back into their rhythm within 24-48 hours. If you're travelling in the middle of the day, try to keep your baby awake. Maintain the two-hour nap/two hours awake schedule. If you're travelling at night, try to transfer your baby to their crib when you arrive.

The normal wake up time should be maintained regardless of how much sleep they've had. They may have additional naps if needed. Feedings should also be maintained; baby should be woken up if needed. Most babies fully adjust to the next time zone within 24-48 hours.

Can I sleep train my older baby while room sharing?

Absolutely. Parents will need to be more disciplined and will need to temporarily adjust their behavior to help their baby. Training should proceed normally. The only real difference is that parents need to make allowances for the realities of room sharing, i.e. added noise, lights, movement, etc. Hence, parents must be even more disciplined. Stick to the training rules very consistently to see results. If you are training a baby older than 10 months, you may leave the room if the crying is too intense. Parents should reenter when their baby is calmer or asleep.

How do I handle vacations?

Enjoy yourself! Vacations are a great opportunity for your baby to learn to be flexible. The number one rule is to have fun! Pay attention to your baby's cues near nap time. Parents should be ready with a suitable nap location, such as under an umbrella at the beach, a cushion at the pool, etc. Vacations are tiring, be flexible here as well. You can very safely put your baby to bed early or later than usual if necessary.

Don't worry about losing the progress you've made. If you go back to their schedule within 48 hours of arriving back home your baby should go back to normal with ease.

I need my older toddler and my newborn to share a room, how do I sleep train without disturbing my toddler?

We recommend that you sleep train your baby in another room, especially if your toddler has great sleeping habits. Once your baby is sleeping consistently for at least a week, you can begin to put them to sleep in the shared bedroom.

We find that putting your baby to bed 30 minutes before your toddler will help to make this transition easier on the toddler. This will give them some one on one time with parents, as well as teaching them to be respectful and considerate of their younger sibling.

You can do both nighttime routines at the same time. Once you've put your baby to bed you can exit the room with your toddler for extra books or songs. Once your baby is older than 18 months, you can begin to put both toddlers to bed at the same time.

We're moving soon, how will that affect sleep training?

If you're just beginning the sleep training process and are set to move within a month, we recommend delaying sleep training. If your move is more than a